SHEKINAH GLORY

LED BY THE CLOUD

A CLOUD BY DAY! A FIRE BY NIGHT!

MARY DONNA HANKLA

Book Cover by Sermonassist

Illustrations by Katerina R.

1st edition 2024

ISBN: 979-8-9880394-4-0

Library of Congress Control Number: 2024912308

DEDICATION

I am grateful for all the people God has brought into my life to encourage me to seek the Scriptures. When I was a teenager, Larry and Kay Smith were my 4-H leaders. In addition to teaching us about 4-H, they taught us the Bible. Those Bible stories really inspired me!

This book is dedicated to young people and all who want to be led by God. Many people immediately type in their questions to search engines, trusting that these sources will give them the right answers. But they are sadly missing the best guidance of all: the instructions of the Holy Spirit.

I dedicate this book to my husband, Kenneth Hankla, and my son, Chris Hankla. Both have stood by me in this pursuit to write. Kenny provides encouragement, while Chris is the glue that brings the book together. Chris also provides technical support and ensures a successful book launch.

Katrina Sheffield, my niece, is a very loyal supporter whom I can count on!

I express gratitude for all who support me in prayer, with much thanks to Ron and Sandra Fowler for their constant encouragement. Also, I appreciate my prayer partner, Libby Repass.

CONTENTS

Foreword 9

Introduction 13

Chapter 1 – His Ways Are Higher 17

Chapter 2 – God's Timing: Wins Spiritual Battles 39

Chapter 3 – Shekinah Cloud Leads the March 61

Chapter 4 – Game Changer Spiritual Weapons: Part 1 ...83

Chapter 5 – Game Changer Spiritual Weapons: Part 2 103

Chapter 6 – Prophesy to the Wind 125

Chapter 7 – Signs and Wonders 147

Chapter 8 – Keys to Open Heaven 171

About the Author 185

FOREWORD

I have known Mary Donna Hankla for several years. I find her to be a woman of prayer and faith. Her books inspire us to walk closer to God each day.

This book, *Shekinah Glory: Led by the Cloud*, will help us understand how God leads His people and will give greater insight into His Word. I am sure it will be a blessing to all who read it and will bring us spiritual renewal and refreshing. I highly recommend this book to all!

Ronald Fowler
Served as Pastor–Evangelist
Served as WIN Prayer Director

I have known Donna for 20 years. She is the most faithful prayer partner anyone could ever have. We pray together six days a week in the mornings.

Donna truly is an intercessor. God surely leads our day just like He did the children of Israel with a cloud by day and a fire by night. You will see this in her book, *Shekinah Glory Led by the Cloud.*

This God-breathed book is going to enlighten you to live victoriously and grow spiritually. It will help you know God more intimately as you read each chapter!

Sandra Fowler
Served as WIN Director
Upper South Carolina Conference, IPHC

I met Ron and Sandra Fowler during a WIN (Worldwide Intercessory Network) event in Pigeon Forge, Tennessee. This was an inspiring meeting that featured famous prayer leaders. For me, it was life-changing. The teaching sessions ignited a fire in my soul to pursue intercession more consistently.

After one session, I walked to a Bob Evans restaurant for lunch. We only had one hour to eat but divine connections were made during that time.

Ron and Sandra Fowler were sitting at a table when I walked in. They invited me to eat with them. Immediately, we connected. We were able to talk and pray. They were serving as WIN Prayer Directors with the South Carolina Conference. I was serving as WIN Director of the Appalachian Conference.

This connection has lasted many years.

Ron and Sandra have ministered at the Big 4 P.H. Church several times. And they take time to pray when I call. We pray together every day of the week, except for Sundays. Every morning, we pray for various needs and for God's purposes to be fulfilled.

Mary Donna Hankla

11

INTRODUCTION

Daniel, the Old Testament prophet, unveils an interesting prophecy regarding the end days: knowledge will be increased. He also says that many will run to and fro.

"But thou, O Daniel shut up the words, and seal the book, even to the time of the end: many shall run to and fro, and knowledge shall be increased" (Daniel 12:4 KJV).

Since the time of Daniel, knowledge has increased through various means such as the internet, computers, research, and most recently, artificial intelligence. From the sixth century B.C. onward, access to sources of knowledge has greatly multiplied. In many ways, this increase in knowledge is invaluable. However, most people are quick to search the internet for all answers, including personal concerns.

What happened to the practice of seeking God and receiving instructions from the Holy Spirit?

"But the Comforter, which is the Holy Ghost, whom the Father will send in my name, he shall teach you all things, and bring all things to your remembrance, whatsoever, I have said unto you" (John 14:26 KJV).

While the availability of the internet is desirable and even vital for businesses, can it truly serve as a substitute for seeking God's will?

Searching for answers from the Scriptures and by prayer are proven ways to answer some vital questions. Specific answers that address the needs of an individual are provided by revelation knowledge of the Holy Spirit.

Revelation knowledge is received as we seek God in prayer.

- What gifts has God given me to pursue a career?

- What areas of study should I pursue?

- Which job should I accept?

- Who should I include in my circle of friends?

- What church should I attend?

- Who should I marry?

- Where should I live?

- How can I receive God's wisdom?

- How can I have peace?

- How can I be happy?

- How can I teach my children?

- How can I get out of debt?

As you read this book, you will learn how to tap into the wisdom of God, find answers to solve difficult problems, and emerge victorious in battles! Moreover, the contrast between the ways of God and the ways of men is revealed within the pages of this book!

God led the children of Israel with a cloud by day and a fire by night (Exodus 40:34-38). He guided Moses through an encounter with a burning bush that was not consumed (Exodus 3:1-5). The kings of ancient Israel were led by words from prophets. Jesus was led by the Holy Spirit into the wilderness (Matthew 4:1). The Holy Spirit directed apostle Paul to various regions to preach the gospel (Acts 16:4-5). Likewise, God can lead you in the right direction with the right people.

"When he has brought all his own sheep outside, he walks on ahead of them, and the sheep follow him because they know his voice and recognize his call" (John 10:4 AMP).

"They will never follow a stranger, but will run away from him, because they do not know the voice of strangers" (John 10:5 AMP).

HIS WAYS ARE HIGHER

When seeking personal direction for your life, the very best instructions will come from the Holy Spirit. As you ask Him to guide you and provide instructions, you open doors for the Divine. By inviting the Holy Spirit to intervene, you have welcomed the opportunity for the very best results. If you invite Him to accompany you on your journey, you will not be disappointed.

"For My thoughts are not your thoughts, neither are your ways my ways, saith the Lord. For as the heavens are higher than the earth, so are my ways higher than your ways, and my thoughts than your thoughts" (Isaiah 55:8-9 KJV).

He begins a good work in you, and He completes it. His good work starts in your affairs when you extend an invitation with prayer.

"I am convinced and confident of this very thing, that He who has begun a good work in you will (continue to perfect and complete it until the day of Christ Jesus (the time of His return)" (Philippians 1:6 AMP).

As leaders in ministry or business, we must realize that our decisions impact many people. Incorrect advice or teaching can lead people down the wrong paths, and we are partially responsible. Yes, their choices also play a role in the outcomes, whether good or bad. However, the words that they hear from the leader are influential.

This is why apostle John advises us to test the spirits. Do not believe everything you hear! Take time to pray about what was spoken and to search for scriptures regarding the issue.

"Beloved do not believe every spirit (speaking through a self-proclaimed prophet): instead test the spirits to see whether they are of God because many false prophets and teachers have gone out into the world" (1 John 4:1 AMP).

"For My thoughts are not your thoughts, neither are your ways my ways, saith the Lord." - Isaiah 55: 8,9

"For as the heavens are higher than the earth, so are my ways higher than your ways, and my thoughts than your thoughts." - Isaiah 55: 8,9

WHAT DOES THIS MEAN?

Young people today have been taught how to operate and use computers to find answers. They can simply search for personal answers. However, the question remains: are those answers tailored to their personal needs? Can those answers be trusted?

In the last few years, false teachers and prophets have snatched the spotlight with luring techniques to attract vulnerable listeners!

False prophets confidently share visions and advice that hold no merit. God did not communicate these things to them. By invoking God's name in such a manner, they subject themselves to judgment and entice listeners.

Jeremiah the prophet issued warnings about false prophets.

"Thus says the Lord of hosts, Hearken not unto the words of the prophets that prophesy unto you; they make you vain: they speak a vision of their own heart, and not out of the mouth of the Lord" (Jeremiah 23:17 KJV).

Careless and false words that are released on the Internet worldwide provoke the anger of the Lord.

"Behold, I am against them that prophesy false dreams, saith the Lord, and do tell them, and cause

*my people to err by their lies, and by their lightness;
yet I sent them not, nor commanded them; therefore
they shall not profit this people at all, saith the Lord"*
(Jeremiah 23:32 AMP).

In my opinion, the American church suffered during
the COVID-19 shutdowns by turning to the internet
for spiritual inspiration, only to find a multitude of
false teachers and prophets.

After the COVID-19 shutdowns, the American
church had to regain the trust of its members. It had
to work hard to encourage them to return to the
church setting. As well noted, many churches had to
shut their doors during the COVID-19 period, and
many lost faithful members. Several pastors have
found rebuilding the church after COVID-19 to
be difficult.

THE PERFECT SECOND CAR!

There was a time in my life when I put a lot of miles
on my car due to job demands. My husband and I
both agreed that we needed a reliable second-hand
car.

We were drawn to an ad in the local newspaper that
suggested an elderly person needed to sell a car.
Some of the statements in the ad attracted us to view
the car: it stayed in the garage most of the time. The
elderly man did not drive the car very often. Even

22

when he did drive, he only went short distances. The car received regular oil changes and maintenance. With great expectations, we looked at the car and drove it a short distance. The body of the car was in good shape; the mileage was low, and it appeared to have received good care. The inside was also in good shape and had plenty of room. We drove the car several miles and liked it. For a few thousand dollars, we could have the car, and the title was also available. Finally, we could own a second-hand vehicle! There was one thing that we forgot to do: pray about the decision. In all of our excitement, the one thing that could have saved us from undue suffering was prayer!

TAKE TIME TO PRAY

Within a month, the car demonstrated its age. I was at a client's house performing an in-home visit. When I finished the visit, I found that the car had lost vast amounts of water. Fortunately, Mom had a skilled teenage son whose dad had taught him some car repair skills. The son was able to pour water into my car and get me on my way. This patch repair got me home safely! It turned out that a valve was old and had torn. The car literally could not go a month without some unforeseen problem. And the problems were expensive.

Another time while driving, I heard a knocking sound

around the right front tire. This concerned me because I did not want to get stranded in some of the dangerous areas that I traveled. The repair shop informed me that I needed a new "bearing" for the tire. Again, this was a costly repair for me. On another trip to a client's house, I heard several noises coming from the tires. The car repair shop informed me that I had some "struts" that needed attention. Again, I faced another costly repair bill.

Several times, I realized that my failure to take the time to pray about this car had cost me much in terms of money and repair visits.

I remembered times on the farm with my grandfather. He taught me to drive. He was patient and brave. He would put me in the car and say, "Drive around this field." During our driving times, he offered invaluable advice that I gladly received.

Donna, do not believe everything you hear!

ENOUGH OF THIS CAR

I informed my husband that it was time to get rid of the car, and I wasn't willing to wait very long. I wanted to look out my window and see it was gone! Fortunately, my husband was able to trade the car, bringing relief to our family.

LESSONS LEARNED

Of course, I learned to pray about decisions. There's a scripture that stood out to me, reinforcing this lesson. It's become a passage I turn to practically every day.

"Commit your way unto the Lord; trust also in him; and he shall bring it to pass" (Psalm 37:5 KJV).

My prayer for decisions goes something like this: "Father, I commit this decision to You. Holy Spirit, guide and direct me in the right way."

Lesson two related to being a minister. I realized that when I spoke to people, I had to be accurate. My job required me to preach, teach, write, pray, and at times prophesy. Before delivering any message, I pray about every word. I am careful not to add unnecessary content to the sermon, nor do I want to drag it out. Additionally, I encourage listeners to study the message for themselves.

A CLOUD BY DAY!
A PILLAR OF FIRE BY NIGHT!

GPS navigation systems are readily available for most of us. Automatically, we enter the car and engage the GPS system. A map flashes on the car's dashboard, and a voice provides directions.

When the Israelites made their exodus from Egypt,

they were not alone. God led them both day and night. During the day, He led them with a pillar of cloud. This glowing cloud was the shekinah glory of Yahweh. Years later, when the tabernacle was built, a cloud of God's glory filled it. And when King Solomon built the majestic temple, God's glorious cloud filled it (1 Kings 8:10 KJV). During the night, God led them with a pillar of fire. This supernatural appearance provided light and comfort for God's people during the night.

"And the Lord went before them by day in a pillar of a cloud, to lead them the way; and by night in a pillar of fire, to give them light, to go by day and night" (Exodus 13:21 KJV).

God's glorious cloud continued with them. Imagine waking up in the morning and seeing that pillar of cloud. And then laying down at night beholding the sight of the pillar of fire.

"He took not away the pillar of the cloud by day, nor the pillar of fire by night, from before the people" (Exodus 13:22 KJV).

The cloud was unique in that it was dark on one side and luminous on the other. These features allowed it to give light to the entire camp of Israel. Also, it served as a barrier separating the Israelite camps from those of their enemies, the Egyptians.

PROTECTION FOR THE DAY

From the moment the children of Israel departed from Egypt, God directed and guided them. He led them from the land of bondage, through the wilderness to the Promised Land with supernatural wonders!

A cloud by day, known as the pillar of cloud, led them as they journeyed. This pillar was not just a symbol but also a phenomenon! For forty years through the wilderness, this pillar of cloud led the children of Israel. Until they entered the Promised Land, it went before them. Moreover, the pillar of cloud served as a testimony to other nations of God's special protection over the children of Israel.

The pillar of cloud caused great distress and discomfort to the Egyptians. It even stood between the Egyptians and the nation of Israel. The Egyptians could not touch the children of Israel because the pillar of cloud forbade them.

"And it came to pass, that in the morning watch the Lord looked unto the host of the Egyptians through the pillar of fire and of the cloud and troubled the host of the Egyptians" (Exodus 14:24 KJV).

"And the angel of God, which went before the camp of Israel, removed and went behind them; and the pillar of the cloud went from before their face, and

28

stood behind them. And it came between the camp of the Egyptians and the camp of Israel, and it was a cloud and darkness to them, but it gave light by night to these: so that the one came not near the other all the night" (Exodus 14:19-20 AMP).

The pillar is a symbol of God's faithfulness and a reminder that He does not leave us.

"Let your conversation be without covetousness; and be content with such things as you have: for he has said, I will never leave you, nor forsake you" (Hebrews 13:5 KJV).

The pillar of cloud is also a military tactic to hide us from our enemies. King David was well aware of God's ability to hide him from his enemies. Several times, King Saul hunted him but was not able to touch him, for he was protected by God.

"Thou art my hiding place; thou shalt preserve me from trouble; thou shalt compass me about with songs of deliverance" (Psalm 32:7 KJV).

Of great interest, both ancient and modern armies have utilized dust as part of their military strategies. The use of dust for physical advantages in warfare has been reported by numerous ancient generals. King David makes reference to dust in war:

"Then I did beat them small as the dust before the

wind: I did cast them out as the dirt in the streets"
(Psalm 18:42 KJV).

Another reference is found where King David prays
for victory over his enemies.

*"Let them be as chaff before the wind: and let the
angel of the Lord chase them"* (Psalm 35:5 KJV).

In the book of Job, the evil attacks against Job come
to an end when God appears as a whirlwind that scatters his enemies. After God appears in the whirlwind,
the situation turns in Job's favor.

*"Then the Lord answered Job out of the whirlwind,
and said, Who is this that darkens counsel by words
without knowledge? Gird up now your loins like a
man; for I will demand of thee, and answer thou me"*
(Job 38:1-3 KJV).

Confirmation of the whirlwind is provided in the
book of Proverbs.

*"As the whirlwind passes, so is the wicked no more;
but the righteousness is an everlasting foundation"*
(Proverbs 10:25 KJV).

One example of an ancient general is noted in his-
tory. The great general named Hannibal was clever.
He created clouds of dust to blind his enemies. Prior
to the battle, he had the site plowed so that the soil
would be very sandy. Loose soil was left on top of

the ground. He knew that the winds blew in the direction of the battle site around noon during the summer. He positioned his army so that the wind would be at their backs. Then he lured the enemy to attack in the direction that the wind would blow. During the battle, the wind came down with great force like a hurricane. Dust blew into the eyes of the Roman soldiers, and the winds whipped them. The wind also choked them. They were so disabled that they succumbed to Hannibal's army.

THE PILLAR OF CLOUD FOR US

Our enemies are not flesh and blood; rather, they are principalities and powers. Therefore, our weapons must be effective prayer. We must pray for God to intervene. We can pray for angels to assist. We can pray for wisdom. We can pray for God's strategies to be released. Our prayers can open doors for heaven to intervene on our behalf! Our prayers can bring angels on the scene.

> *Finally, my brethren, be strong in the Lord, and in the power of his might. Put on the whole armor of God, that you may be able to stand against the wiles of the devil. For we wrestle not against flesh and blood, but against principalities, against powers, against the rulers of darkness of this world,*

against spiritual wickedness in high places. (Ephesians 6:10-12 KJV)

PILLAR OF FIRE BY NIGHT

And they took their journey from Succoth, and encamped in Etham, in the edge of the wilderness. And the Lord went before them by day in a pillar of a cloud to lead them the way; and by night in a pillar of fire, to give them light; to go by day and night! (Exodus 13:20-21 KJV)

This pillar of fire also guided the children of Israel through the wilderness, assured them of God's presence, and protected them from their enemies. Fire in the Scriptures refers to purging and destruction. God's pillar of fire went before the children of Israel and scattered their enemies. Fire is a noted characteristic of God.

"For our God is a consuming fire" (Hebrews 12:29 KJV).

During the night, the children of Israel could look outside their tents and see the pillar of fire. Then they could lie back down to sleep with assurance that God was protecting them. Likewise, we can be assured that God's presence will watch over us at night. Our prayers at night invite Him to do so.

"I will both lay me down in peace, and sleep: for thou, Lord, only makes me dwell in safety" (Psalm 4:8 KJV).

HIS EYES OF FIRE

One night, I attended a revival meeting at a church that held prayer meetings for the city of Bluefield, WV. I recall the message of the pastor. He challenged us to build our lives on the firm foundation of Jesus Christ. This required prayer, Bible study, and commitment. I was already very hungry for the presence of God. Once you have felt His peace and joy, you long for more!

> *For other foundation can no man lay than that is laid, which is Jesus Christ. Now if any man build upon this foundation gold, silver, precious stones, wood, hay, stubble. Every man's work shall be made manifest: for the day shall declare it, because it shall be revealed by fire; and the fire shall try every man's work of what sort it is.* (1 Corinthians 3:11-13 KJV)

Suddenly, I saw Jesus with His eyes of fire. The face was just above the pulpit at the front of the church. His eyes gazed upon the congregation, directly reaching their hearts. My heart was also within His line of sight!

Those eyes of fire provided timely direction for my life. My eyes were fixed on this supernatural scene. At this point, I knew that I was called to the ministry of prayer. I would pray for people, churches, cities, regions, and even nations! I would engage in all-night prayer watches and 24-hour prayer watches!

"His head and his hairs were white like wool, as white as snow, and his eyes were as a flame of fire" (Revelation 1:14 KJV).

SIGNIFICANCE OF THE PILLAR OF CLOUD AND THE PILLAR OF FIRE

1. A compass to lead the children of Israel through the wilderness.

   "I will instruct you and teach you in the way which you should go: I will guide you with mine eye" (Psalm 32:8 AMP).

2. God's directive was revealed.

   "Moses and Aaron among his priests, and Samuel among them that call upon his name; they called upon the Lord, and he answered them, He spoke unto them in the cloudy pillar: they kept his testimonies, and the ordinance that he gave them" (Psalm 99:6-7 KJV).

3. Security and protection were provided for the children of Israel.

    Other nations saw the pillar of cloud by day and the pillar of fire by night, and fear struck their hearts. They knew that Israel had supernatural protection.

    We are also assured of protection through the Lord's Prayer. We can pray these words over our lives.

    "And lead us not into temptation, but deliver us from evil: For thine is the kingdom, and the power, and the glory, forever, Amen" (Matthew 6:13 KJV).

4. A sign of God's power was indeed a feature. Imagine this nation of Israelites traveling through the wilderness. Before them is a pillar of cloud by day and at night, a pillar of fire. These reminders of God's presence assured the children of Israel and brought terror to their enemies!

    "And they will tell it to the inhabitants of this land: for they have heard that thou Lord art among this people, that thou Lord art seen face to face, and that thy cloud standeth over them, and that thou goest before them, by day time in

a pillar of a cloud, and in a pillar of fire by night" (Numbers 14:14 KJV).

God's protection is also for you!

"The angel of the Lord encamps round about them that fear him, and delivers them" (Psalm 34:7 KJV).

2

GOD'S TIMING: WINS SPIRITUAL BATTLES

Successful military strategies include the timing of attacks. Timing can be the difference between victory or defeat. Both ancient and modern armies consider timing to be a key factor for victory. For this reason, intelligence gathering is often performed to determine the best time to attack. Both the pillar of cloud by day and the pillar of fire by night provided the children of Israel with cues on when to go and when to stay.

> *And when the cloud was taken up from the tabernacle, then after that the children of Israel journeyed: and in the place where the cloud abode, there the children of Israel pitched their tents. At the commandment of the Lord the children of Israel journeyed, and at the commandment of the Lord they pitched: as long as the cloud abode upon the tabernacle they rested in their tents.* (Numbers 9:17-18 KJV)

THE STORY OF THE MISSIONARIES

This testimony of several missionaries had a major impact on me. This testimony confirmed to me that it is important to be in the right place at the right time!

These missionaries had a secret meeting place where they met daily for prayer. They did not tell anyone the time of the daily meetings. Rather, each person spent time in prayer and listened to the leading of the Holy Spirit. These missionaries met at the same time each day under the direction of the Holy Spirit!

One day, another person joined their ranks. They suspected him to be a spy. Eagerly, he asked for the time of the next meeting as he intended to bring the police to arrest these zealous Christians. They told him that he would have to receive the time from the Holy Spirit. He would have to pray and listen.

The next meeting was held and everyone was present at the correct time except for this spy. He was not able to listen to the directions of the Holy Spirit!

SHOW YOURSELF TO AHAB

Elijah, the prophet, was in tune with God's timing. A drought had come upon the land of Israel as part of God's judgment. The word of the Lord came to Elijah. He was instructed to hide at the brook of Cherith. He was told to drink from the water of the brook. And at God's command, ravens brought him bread and meat in the morning and the evening (1 Kings 17:2-6).

This was a comfortable place for Elijah. It provided safety and food for him. However, the drought became severe. The brook dried up. God's word again came to Elijah. He was instructed to go to Zarephath. He was to meet a widow there. She would take care of him (1 Kings 17:8-9).

When he got to the town, he met the widow. However, she was in such distress that she was preparing her last meal for herself and her son. Elijah asked her to give him a morsel of bread and some water. She told him that she only had two sticks. She was preparing to cook the sticks and serve it to herself and her son, and then die. What a meal! What a plan! (1 Kings 17:12).

Elijah encouraged her to respond in faith. She brought him a cake first. When she handed the cake to him, the miracle began. Miraculously, her jar of flour began to fill up, and her jug of oil filled up. Her family would survive the famine! (1 Kings 17:14-16).

The day came when God told Elijah to show himself to King Ahab. For a long time, the prophet had remained hidden from the evil king. But God's timing was crucial to restoring rain to the nation of Israel.

"And it came to pass after many days, that the word of the Lord came to Elijah in the third year, saying, Go show yourself unto Ahab; and I will send rain upon the earth" (1 Kings 18:1 KJV).

This is a lesson regarding the right time to come before people of high standing such as employers, government leaders, and even rulers of nations!

This is a lesson that served me well when scheduling a key job interview.

FLY FISHING

I learned about the importance of timing during fly fishing trips with my dad. I watched him tie the flies at his home desk. Each fly was effective at certain times. Wet flies were used underwater and dry flies were used on top of the water. The rainbow trout were attracted to these flies, especially if they were carefully jerked upstream, and other times allowed to float downstream.

The Woolly Bugger fly was one of Dad's favorites. This fly belongs to the class of flies known as streamers. It imitates crayfish, minnows, leeches, and other natural foods that native trout love! This fly is used in late fall after the fish spawn and throughout the winter. Dawn is a desired time to lure a trout with this fly. Dusk is another time when trout show interest in this fly.

Next, there was the caddis fly. It was popular in the spring, especially during the month of April. Most caddisflies lay their eggs in the late afternoon. Within hours, the flies emerge and hover over the stream. I loved this fly. I caught a lot of trout during the late afternoons and early evenings with the caddis fly.

The Adams fly was one of the most successful flies. When other trout flies or bait did not work, we could count on the Adams fly. It is a dry fly primarily used for trout. I recall many times just before dusk, floating this fly on the stream. The fish would come to the top of the water to grab flies, so I made sure my fly was among the natural ones.

Finally, there was the Royal Coachman. I have to say that this is my favorite fly. During the months of July and August, I headed to our favorite stream. I hid behind a bush and floated my dry fly down the stream. And often, I was rewarded. The rainbow trout would rush toward the fly and drag it under the water. The fight was on. I had to play with the fish. But I could not pull too hard, or the fish would break the line. The timing of success with this fly, for me, was at early dawn and dusk.

TO EVERYTHING THERE IS A SEASON

Maybe you have heard the song, "Turn, Turn, Turn" by the Byrds. It is a song that has inspired me. I love the tune and the lyrics. The words are taken from the book of Ecclesiastes in the Bible.

> *To everything there is a season, and a time to every purpose under the heaven. A time to be born, and a time to die; a time to plant, and a time to pluck up that which is planted. A time to kill, and a time to heal; a time to break down, and a time to build up; A time to weep, and a time to laugh; a time to mourn, and a time to dance; A time cast away stones, and a time to gather stones together, a time to embrace, and a time to refrain from embracing. A time to get, a time to lose; a time to keep, and a time to cast away. A time to rend, and a time to sew; a time to keep silence, and a time to speak; A time to love, and a time of hate; a time of war, and a time of peace.* (Ecclesiastes 3:1-9 KJV)

IN GOD'S HANDS

King David learned to trust God, even with his life. The former King Saul had chased him and his men, hunting them. King Saul made many efforts to kill David because he was insanely jealous.

I love reading the story of David's life. It reveals just how powerful God's hand of protection is during times of imminent danger. King Saul could not harm David because, before King Saul could strike a final blow, David mysteriously disappeared.

Recall the time when David and his men escaped into the wilderness. He had about 600 men with him. King Saul could not harm David and his men!

"And David abode in the wilderness in strongholds, and remained in a mountain in the wilderness of Ziph. And Saul sought him every day, but God delivered him not into his hand" (1 Samuel 23:14 KJV).

And that is not the end of the story. King Saul and his men came very close to David in the wilderness. They went to one side of the mountain, while David and his men escaped to the other side. King Saul and his men were getting closer to David and his band of men. But suddenly, a messenger came to King Saul. The message was to hurry back because the Philistines had invaded the land (1 Samuel 23:27).

48

THE PRAYER OF TIMES

There is a scripture that can be prayed. It was written by David who knew God's faithfulness to protect.

"My times are in thy hand: deliver me from the hand of mine enemies, and from them that persecute me" (Psalm 31:15 KJV).

The Hebrew name for God as a protector is *Magen*, which refers to the Lord as my shield. God can shield you and your family from danger. Even in the Lord's Prayer, Jesus emphasizes that we can ask for God's protection.

"And lead us not into temptation, but deliver us from evil: for thine is the kingdom, and the power, and the glory, forever. Amen" (Matthew 6:13 KJV).

UNDERSTANDING OF THE TIMES

During the reign of King David, there was one tribe that was credited with having the ability to discern the times. Because of this ability, they were able to make the right decisions.

"And of the children of Issachar, which were men that had understanding of the times, to know what Israel ought to do; the heads of them were two hundred; and all their brethren were at their commandment" (1 Chronicles 12:32 KJV).

FACTS ABOUT ISSACHAR

The tribe of Issachar inspires God's people to pursue His gifts of understanding and knowledge. The wisdom and knowledge of the world are inferior to God's wisdom. We must not neglect to seek God's wisdom and pray for His understanding. Scriptures suggest that the wisdom of the world is tainted with envy, jealousy, and even strife.

"But if you have bitter envying, strife in your hearts, glory not, and lie not against the truth" (James 3:14 KJV).

"This wisdom descends not from above, but is earthy, sensual, devilish" (James 3:15 KJV).

Indeed, the Devil has wisdom to impart, and demonic spirits delight in those who seek this wisdom, rather than God's wisdom. Jesus referred to this fact when He told the disciples to be wise as serpents but gentle as doves (Matthew 10:16).

Be very careful in your search for wisdom!

"But the wisdom that is from above is first pure, then peaceable, gentle, and easy to be entreated, full of mercy, and good fruits, without partiality, and without hypocrisy" (James 3:17 KJV).

The descendants of the tribe of Issachar were primarily scholars. They are even credited with creating the Israelite calendar. For these reasons, they were invaluable to

King David as they had an understanding of the times and knew what actions the nation should take!

STOP! DO NOT PROCEED UNTIL
YOU ASK FOR HIS WISDOM!

You do not have to wait until the end of this book to receive God's wisdom. This gift is ready to be released as you ask in prayer. In my life, there have been many times when I needed God's wisdom. Some situations were so dire that life and death hung in the balance.

When I was just a young child in elementary school, I became extremely ill in a short amount of time. Symptoms of weakness, nausea, and abdominal cramps were severe. Alarmed, my mother took me to the doctor. This was not just any doctor. He was a man of prayer who acknowledged God's wisdom. As I lay there, I heard the doctor say, "Stay here. I will be back in a few minutes." He went to a private room to pray.

Then he reviewed my lab results and determined that I had salmonella. It was transmitted to me by a recent pet turtle. The doctor instructed the nurses to administer the correct medicines into my system immediately. Within an hour, I was on my feet and asking for a hamburger! At an early age, I was aware that God's wisdom was available.

MY PRAYER! YOUR PRAYER!

For years, I prayed a prayer that the apostle Paul wrote to the church of Ephesus. And I still pray it frequently.

> *(I always pray) that the God of our Lord Jesus Christ, the Father of glory, may grant you a spirit of wisdom and of revelation (that gives you a deep and personal and intimate insight) into the true knowledge of Him (for we know the Father through the Son). And I pray that the eyes of your heart (the very center and core of you being) may be enlightened (flooded with light by the Holy Spirit), so that you will know and cherish the hope (the divine guarantee, the confident expectation) to which He has called you, the riches of His glorious inheritance, in the saints (God's people).*
> (Ephesians 1:17-18 AMP)

FASCINATING FACTS

Issachar featured a famous biblical genealogy. He was the great-grandson of Abraham, the father of faith (Galatians 3:6-9).

He was the grandson of Isaac. Issachar was Jacob's ninth son. Leah was his mother (Genesis 30:5-21). At his death, Jacob gave a special prophetic blessing to each of his twelve sons.

"Then Jacob called for his sons and said, "Assemble yourselves (around me) that I may tell you what will happen to you and your descendants in the days to come" (Genesis 49:1 AMP).

"Issachar is (like) a strong–boned donkey, crouching down between the sheepfolds. When he saw that the resting place was good and that the land was pleasant, he bowed his shoulder to bear (burdens) and became a servant at forced labor" (Genesis 49:14-15 AMP).

Thus, the times and purposes of Issachar were prophesied!

When Joshua led the people into the Promised Land and gave allotments to each tribe, Issachar was among them (Joshua 19: 17-23). The fourth lot went to the tribe of Issachar. Their border reached Tabor and Beth-shemesh and ended at the Jordon River. Included were sixteen cities and their villages.

The strong donkey phrase suggests a tribe that would labor and become prosperous. The resting place and pleasant land describe the location that the tribe would occupy.

Once the children of Israel settled in the Promised Land of Canaan, the tribe of Issachar received allotted boundaries in a fertile land, in the central realms of the region. The people of Issachar became prosperous from their manual labor, working the land. They became the third most populous of the tribes.

SYMBOL FOR ISSACHAR

There are two notable symbols for this tribe. Because Issachar was born to Leah, Jacob's second wife, this Hebrew name was chosen. Rachel was Jacob's first wife but her womb was barren. She could not have children. In her distress, she urged Jacob to engage with Leah. And the child would be hers.

This night of engagement led to Issachar's birth. His Hebrew name referred to reward. He was birthed by hire (labor) and brought reward. The people of the tribe of Issachar were known to be hard workers and prosperous. The prophecy in Genesis Chapter 49 portrayed them as a donkey, hardworking (Genesis 49:14-15):

"Issachar is (like) a strong-boned donkey, couching down between the sheepfolds. When he saw that the resting place was pleasant, He bowed his shoulder to bear burdens. And became a servant at forced labor" (AMP)

In the center of the flag is a picture of a donkey with heavy packs on it. They are strong people, able to carry heavy burdens.

The second symbol featured a bluish-black flag with a sun and a moon. These symbols relate to the fact that they understood the times. They were wise in astronomical and chronological bodies of knowledge.

DO YOU HAVE THE MARK OF WISDOM?

Are you spending time in prayer seeking God's instructions? Are you taking the time to commit your ways to God?

"Commit your way to the Lord; trust in Him also and He will do it" (Psalm 37:5 AMP).

Do you believe that God can release answers to you that will solve difficult problems?

God helped the prophet Daniel solve tough problems, and He will do the same for you!

"It was because an extraordinary spirit, knowledge and insight, the ability to interpret dreams, clarify riddles, and solve complex problems were found in Daniel, whom the king named Belteshazzar. Now let Daniel be called and he will give the interpretation" (Daniel 5:12 AMP).

Daniel was marked by wisdom that surpassed the knowledge of the nation of Babylon.

Take your fingers off the search key and lift them toward heaven!

SHEKINAH CLOUD LEADS THE MARCH

Imagine that you are sitting on a hill watching the tribes of Israel prepare to march. The dark night has ended, and the light of dawn shatters the darkness. You see the cloud by day blazing brightly. The pillar of cloud begins to move from its position over the tabernacle. Several people open the doors of their tents and view this supernatural sign. Others alert the tribes. They shout, "The cloud is moving."

THE SHEKINAH GLORY CLOUD

Your eyes are glued on the fiery cloud hovering over the ark of the tabernacle. High in the sky, the fiery light flashes. It is a breathtaking sight. For miles, it can be seen!

This is the cloud that will lead the nation. It will go before the nation and do other vital things.

- During the night (a time noted for spiritual battle), the pillar of fire burns vehemently. It provides protection from lurking enemies.

  Likewise, the Holy Spirit protects us during the night hours. His very presence scatters the enemies.

- The cloud provided a covering of spiritual protection for the people.

  "And the lord went before them by day in a pillar of a cloud to lead them the way; and by

62

night in a pillar of fire, to give them light; to go by day and night" (Exodus 13:21 KJV).

- The fiery cloud frightened the enemies of the nation. Fear struck their hearts when they saw this supernatural phenomenon!

- The cloud was a reminder to the nation that God had delivered them from the bondage of Egypt.

- The high priests witnessed the cloud between the two cherubim angels when they performed their priestly duties. They confirmed to the nation that God's presence had chosen to appear. Yes, God's presence was still with the nation!

"There I will meet with you; from above the mercy seat, from between the two cherubims which are on the ark of the testimony, I will speak (intimately) with you regarding every commandment that I will give you for the Israelites" (Exodus 25:22 AMP).

THE SHEKINAH GLORY TODAY

This Hebrew word, *shekinah,* refers to dwelling or settling down. Even as God's presence dwelled between the two cherubim, His presence can abide within us. Scripture confirms that since Jesus died on the cross and was resurrected from the dead we can have access to God's Spirit (John 14:6; Romans 5:2 KJV). We can invite the Holy Spirit to lead, teach, and protect us. Look at the New Testament descriptions of the Holy Spirit.

"Do you not know that your body is a temple of the Holy Spirit who is within you, whom you have (received as a gift) from God, and that you are not your own property" (1 Corinthians 6:19 AMP).

A TASTE OF GOD'S GOODNESS FOR ME

The Holy Spirit is one of the greatest gifts that God has given us. The Spirit of God can fill our hearts with great joy, peace, and power. When we enter the cloud, we will not come out the same. This cloud will transform our lives!

Recall Moses coming off Mount Sinai from his meeting with God. He carried the two covenant tablets in his hands. His face shone so brightly that he had to put a veil over it when speaking to the people (Exodus 34:29 -35).

I remember times of His refreshing presence in my life. When I accepted Jesus Christ as my Lord and Savior at the age of seventeen, I received the infilling of the Holy Spirit. However, I wanted to experience His presence. I longed for His joy and peace in the Holy Ghost.

"For the kingdom of God is not meat and drink, but righteousness, and peace, and joy in the Holy Ghost" (Romans 14:17 KJV*)*.

When I read this scripture, I asked the Lord for all of it! I wanted to experience His joy!

As I mentioned in my first book, I attended a prayer group that met in the mornings before the start of classes. Several students raised their hands as they prayed, and they prayed with great confidence. Their faces shone with joy! I wanted to be like that. I asked the students to pray for me. I thought of it as having a full tank of gas.

"And be not drunk with wine, wherin is excess; but be filled with the spirit" (Ephesians 5:18 KJV).

Several students gathered around me and prayed. Their prayers were filled with passion. They sincerely cared about me!

When they finished praying, they asked me if I felt anything. I told them that I did not feel anything.

However, I had faith that I was filled with the Holy Spirit. That night, in my bed, I told the Father that even though I had not felt anything, I still believed I was filled with the Holy Spirit.

The next day at school, I opened my locker and picked up my anatomy book. This would be my first class, and we had a major test. As soon as I opened the locker door, I felt a sudden rush of the wind of the Holy Spirit. This was new to me, and it was awesome. The power of the Holy Spirit was so strong that I had to hang onto my locker for a few minutes.

When I went to take my test, I was surprised. I had studied for the test; however, when I started to answer a question, something happened. A bright light shined upon the correct answers. The next day, I saw a grade of 100 on my test paper!

For three days, I was filled with great peace and joy. And people could see that something was different. My mom asked what was going on with me. I attempted to explain!

You can also experience the supernatural peace and joy of the Holy Spirit.

ENCAMPMENT OF THE TRIBES

The manner in which the tribes encamped was spectacular. In the center of the camp was the tabernacle with the pillar of fire hovering above it.

> *And the children of Israel shall pitch their tents, every man by his own camp, and every man by his own standard, throughout their hosts. But the Levites shall pitch round about the tabernacle of the testimony, that there be no wrath upon the congregation of the children of israel: and the Levites shall keep the charge of the tabernacle of testimony.* (Numbers 1:52-53 KJV)

Back to your hill! As you sat on the hill, you viewed the order of the encampment of the tribes. This formation is important for several reasons. The order of the encampment was directed by God. Moses received these heavenly instructions.

The tabernacle was always at the center of the camp of Israel. The priestly tribe of Levi was assigned to care for the tabernacle and to perform the rituals of worship (Numbers Chapter 2).

Their order of encampment would also dictate their marching positions.

"And the Lord spoke unto Moses and unto Aaron, saying, Every man of the children of Israel shall pitch by his own standard, with the ensign of their father's house: far off about the tabernacle of the congregation shall they pitch" (Numbers 2:1-2 KJV).

"Then the tabernacle of the congregation shall set forward with the camp of the Levites in the midst of the camp: as they encamp, so shall they set forward, every man in his place by their standards" (Numbers 2:17 KJV).

The lesson for us is that we should seek first the kingdom of God (Matthew 6:33).

Also, God demonstrated that He wants to dwell in the midst of His people!

With the tribe of Levi in the center and the other tribes surrounding it, the image of a cross can be imagined. The cross symbolizes God's redemptive plan for us.

POSITIONS OF THE TRIBES

The twelve tribes were divinely arranged in groups of three and situated around the tabernacle. As stated, the Levites were the only tribe allowed to camp somewhat close to the tabernacle. They surrounded the tabernacle on each side: east, west, north, and south. Therefore, they were able to care for the tabernacle and perform the religious rituals.

The tribes of Judah, Issachar, and Zebulun were referred to as the camp of Judah. They encamped on the east of the Levites. To the north of the tabernacle encamped the tribes of Dan, Asher, and Naphtali. To the west of the tabernacle encamped the tribes of Ephraim, Manasseh, and Benjamin. To the south of the tabernacle encamped the tribes of Reuben, Simeon, and Gad. To the east of the tabernacle encamped the tribes of Judah, Issachar, and Zebulun.

This arrangement of camps was clearly organized by the Lord and revealed to Moses. Actually, there are a total of thirteen tribes when the tribe of Levi is included.

ENCAMPMENT OF THE TRIBES

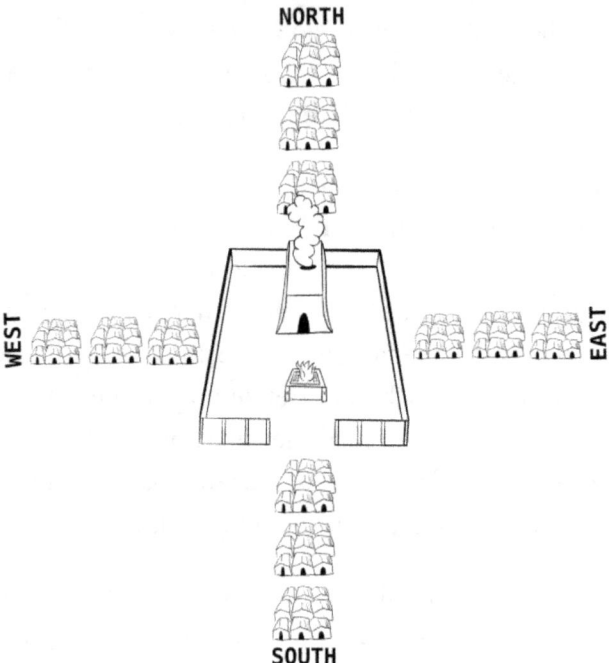

NORTH

WEST

EAST

SOUTH

Numbers 2:1–17
Resembles the shape of the cross

THE SUN IS RISING

From your vantage point atop the hill, you see this divine arrangement of camps. It captures your attention and reminds you that God is a God of order.

"For God is not a God of confusion and disorder but of peace and order" (1 Corinthians 14:33 AMP).

Families are waking up. Tent doors are opening, and fires are being started. The pillar of cloud is hovering over the tabernacle, and many eyes are looking toward it!

THE MARCH BEGINS

Two distinct phases of the march of the children of Israel are mentioned in the Scriptures. Of course, they first marched out of Egypt to the Red Sea. Pharaoh's army pursued them, despite his permission for them to leave.

A great company of Israelites marched out of Egypt. It is estimated that approximately 603,550 Israelite men left (Exodus 38:25-26 KJV). If you consider that each man had a family of at least two children, the number could have been 2,400,000.

And they left with the treasures of Egypt.

> *And the children of Israel did according to the word of Moses; and they*

borrowed of the Egyptians jewels of silver, and jewels of gold, and raiment. And the Lord gave the people favor in the sight of the Egyptians, so they lent unto them such things as they required. And they spoiled the Egyptians. (Exodus 12:35-36 KJV)

Of great amazement, the children of Israel also left in good health.

"He brought them forth also with silver and gold: and there was not a feeble person among their tribes" (Psalm 105:37 KJV).

For 430 years, they had suffered in bondage under the nation of Egypt (Exodus 12:40-41). Now they are standing at the Red Sea wondering how to get across to safety. Behind them, Pharaoh's army threatens. The pillar of cloud did not disappoint. It gave the nation a cover of protection. It literally stood between the nation of Israel and Pharaoh's army!

And the angel of God, which went before the camp of Israel, removed and went behind them; and the pillar of the cloud went from before their face, and stood behind them. And it came between the camp of the Egyptians and the camp of Israel; and it was a cloud and darkness to them, but it

74

gave light by night to these: so that the one came not near the other all the night. (Exodus 14:19-20 KJV)

Suddenly, Moses stretched out his hand (with the rod) over the sea. In response, the Lord caused a strong east wind to blow all night, and the waters divided and created a path. There was a wall of water on one side of the path and a wall of water on the other side of the path (Exodus 14:21-22 KJV).

The Israelites passed over on the dry path!

As soon as they crossed the sea, Moses stretched out his hand again. This time, the waters fell upon Pharaoh's army as they pursued the children of Israel! Not one of Pharaoh's soldiers survived (Exodus 12:28 KJV).

The journey to the Promised Land would soon begin. The first phase would be from Egypt to Horeb. The second phase would be from Horeb to Canaan.

THE PILLAR OF CLOUD IS MOVING

When the cloud moved, the nation moved. When the cloud stayed, the nation stayed (Exodus 40:36-38; Numbers 9:15-18).

The camp of the Levites was close to the tabernacle. The priests watched for the cloud to move so they could alert the rest of the nation. Being close to the

Lord is also important for us. Those who are close to Him will be able to discern divine instructions.

THE CALL TO MARCH

Two silver trumpets were blown to alert the people to prepare to march. These trumpets would coordinate the movements of the tribes as they marched (Numbers 10:4-10 KJV).

On the first blast of the silver trumpets, the tribes that dwelled on the east side of the tabernacle began the march. With the second sound of the trumpet, the tribes on the south side followed. The tribes on the north and west sides of the tabernacle joined ranks at their appointed time. Everything was performed in an orderly fashion! The disciplined manner in which God's army marched is described in the book of Joel.

"They march (straight ahead) in line, and they do not deviate from their paths. They do not crowd each other. Each one marches in his path" (Joel 2:7 AMP).

A spiritual warfare message can be gleaned from the manner of the march. We are to allow God to direct us in our battles. We are to move when He directs and to stay put unless He calls us to a particular battle!

FLAGS OF THE TRIBES

Watching the tribes on the march is a remarkable sight. The cloud of pillar flashes rays of bright light at the front of the march. The ark of the tabernacle is being carried by the priestly tribe of Levi. The flags of every tribe are lifted high during the march. The flags are also referred to as banners. Their descriptions are found in the prophecy of Jacob regarding his sons (Genesis Chapter 49). A brief review of the tribes is described in the books of Genesis and Numbers.

Reuben: this banner is red and embroidered with mandrakes (Genesis 30:14).

- Simeon: a green flag with the town of Shechem featured portrays this flag (Genesis Chapter 34)
  The symbol for this tribe is the sword and the gate (Genesis Chapter 34).
- Levi: this flag or banner is unusual. It is made of three vertical sections with the colors of white, black, and red. At the center is an image of the breastplate of the high priest. This breastplate has three vertical rows that feature the stones of the twelve tribes of Israel (Exodus 28:15-19).
- Judah: this flag is a square with the background of a blue sky, resembling the heavens.

A lion serves as the emblem (Genesis 49:8-9).

- Dan: this flag is a blue square with a serpent as an insignia (Genesis 49:16-17).
- Naphtali: a purple-red square with a hind as the emblem is the flag of this tribe (Genesis 49:21).
- Gad: the square portion is grey with a blend of black and blue sky color. Of great interest, the encampment of the tents is the emblem (Genesis 49:19; Numbers 1:24-25).
- Asher: a woman's turban with the color of bluish-green is fashioned in the shape of a square. An olive tree is the insignia (Genesis 49:20).
- Issachar: this banner includes a donkey as the emblem on the background of the color blue (Genesis 49:14).
- Zebulun: the color of the flag is white and the emblem shown is a ship (Genesis 49:13).
- Joseph: the flag is black with a sheaf of wheat as the insignia (Genesis 49:22).
- Ephraim: the flag is black with the emblem of a bullock (Numbers 1:32-33; Genesis 48:14-20).
- Manasseh: the flag is black with the emblem of a wild ox (Genesis 48:14-22).
- Benjamin: this flag is very unusual. It consists of a combination of all colors of the tribes. It is embroidered with a wolf (Genesis 49:27).

VISION OF THE MARCHING
ARMY OF GOD

In my first book, *In Your Light We See Light*, I shared in depth about this vision. It occurred in the fall. The leaves were full of the colors of red and yellow. The Appalachian Mountain Range surrounding the Emory & Henry College campus looked like a beautifully painted picture.

The evening air was warm, and a breeze was blowing. Our window was open, and fresh air energized us for the night of study ahead. Three of us were roommates and we all had a lot of academic work to achieve. I was studying for an anatomy test scheduled for the following morning. My attention was directed toward the study notes. Darkness occurred around 9:00 p.m. We had dozed off for a nap when suddenly, we were awakened by a brilliant light. It was dark outside. Yet, our room was shining with a heavenly light. There certainly was not an electric light on!

All three of us shared a deep belief in the power of prayer, so we took turns praying out loud. There was no audible voice, but we all sensed that the Holy Spirit had come to visit us, and we were to acknowledge His presence the entire night!

However, we dozed off to sleep again, only to be awakened about midnight. The beds began to shake. This certainly woke us from sleep. After a few minutes, the beds stopped shaking. But the brilliant light remained. It was around midnight when I clearly heard an army marching past our window. The window was still open to allow the autumn air to fill the room. The marching was so loud that I thought the entire campus would hear it. I rushed to the window to look out. I thought I might see the cadets on a training mission. I saw nobody, yet, the marching continued. It lasted for about 30 minutes.

Even though I did not see soldiers, I sensed that spirits were on the march. And they intended for us to be aware of them. I began to pray. I asked the Lord what I was hearing and sensing in the spirit. This is the answer that I perceived: "This is the Army of the Lord. You will join this army in due time. It will be an Army of Intercessors. You will meet many prayer warriors."

Quickly, the hour of 7:00 a.m. arrived. My test was at 8:00 a.m. I grabbed my books and ran to the classroom. Even though I had stayed up all night, I felt refreshed and was able to concentrate on the test. I scored a grade of A, for excellent!

GAME CHANGER SPIRITUAL WEAPONS

PART 1

Have you ever faced a major problem and prayed every prayer you know to pray? Do not give up! You are not alone. I have been in such situations, and there are people in the Bible who have faced impossible odds. Jehovah Gibbor came through for these people and me.

Jehovah Gibbor is a powerful name for God. It means "The Lord Mighty in Battle." Prayer of deliverance is made when you call on the name of Jehovah Gibbor!

"Our Father, who is in Heaven, fight for me. Cause my enemies to scatter. Give me divine help for my situation. Give me strength and wisdom for my battle. Let me see Your mighty hand at work on my behalf."

"Who is this King glory? The Lord strong and mighty, the Lord mighty in battle" (Psalm 24:8 KJV).

MY CHILD IS HAVING TROUBLE BREATHING

I learned about this powerful name during an unexpected crisis.

One night, my son woke me up. I sensed that something was wrong. He was breathing but struggling for air. It was in the wee hours of the morning. I determined to take him to the doctor as soon as we could.

I gave him the prescribed medications and sat by his side. I prayed for wisdom and answers to end this crisis! I prayed in the name of Jesus and declared the blood of Jesus over him. Numerous scriptures were prayed for him. A special scripture from the Psalms was prayed with great passion.

"Then they cry unto the Lord, in their trouble, and he saves them out of their distresses. He sent His Word and healed them, and delivered them from their destructions" (Psalm 107:19-20 KJV).

We arrived at the medical office. The nurses quickly took my child to the doctor. He was suffering from croup. However, his airway had remained open. Treatment was administered, and his breathing improved. Nevertheless, he had to spend a night in the hospital. But God was on time for my child. His peace comforted me during the crisis.

That situation strengthened my faith in the name of Jehovah Gibbor!

WHEN YOU DON'T KNOW WHAT TO DO

The tribe of Issachar was known for its great understanding. They knew what the nation of Israel should do. King David relied on this tribe.

"And of the children of Issachar, which were men that had understanding of the times, to know what

Israel ought to do; the heads of them were two hundred; and all their brethren were at their commandment" (1 Chronicles 12:32 KJV).

There were times when King David called on these men who possessed great wisdom.

TAKE THE HIGH ROAD

I recall a time when I faced a challenging situation at work. I loved the job and enjoyed working with the clients. But one day, there was a demand for me to make a decision. One decision would bring great benefit for me, but on the other hand, it would cause loss to other employees. I had just graduated from ministry school. Finally, I was an ordained minister. My best friend was truly a woman of prayer. This is what she told me: "You do not want to start the ministry in a manner that would cause loss to others. Do the hard thing. Take the high road."

Those words kept ringing in my head: "Take the high road." That meant doing the right thing, even if I encountered some loss.

I also talked to my pastor about the situation. After he prayed for me, he said, "I feel that you should take the high road." And that is what I did! I have never regretted it. The Lord certainly honored my decision.

In the years to follow, the Lord protected me during company layoffs. I was secure. My job was saved, not once, but several times. Each time, I remembered that I had taken the high road. And that is not all; the Lord opened up excellent job opportunities for my husband and my son. Anytime I face a difficult situation, I continue to "take the high road!"

WISDOM IN TIMES OF CRISIS

There were times when I was asked to pray for urgent requests.

Some examples include:

- Praying for friends facing medical concerns
- Praying for those who have lost their jobs
- Praying for loved ones who have gone astray

I found that a more effective way to pray is to ask for wisdom regarding each request. The wisdom of God is available; we just have to ask!

"If any of you lack wisdom, let him ask of God, that gives to all men liberally and upbraids not; and it shall be given to him" (James 1:5 KJV).

If you are not seeing answers to your prayers, do not give up. Just take a different approach. Ask the Holy Spirit to show you how to pray.

PRAYER FOR CHURCH REPAIRS

For years, the church had survived with the repairs of a few men here and there. It stood firm through two major floods. The only real damage was the basement floor. The men were able to replace the floor. There were still several items that needed attention. Nevertheless, I did not sense any urgency to make

89

many expensive changes. One day, a letter arrived from the insurance company. I was shocked when I read it. The Big 4 P.H. Church would not be fully insured unless a new roof was replaced and an over-haul of both bathrooms was performed.

The total cost of the repairs would be over $10,000. Like many churches, The Big 4 P.H. Church was re-covering from the COVID-19 period. I prayed for wisdom and divine connections. Others prayed as well. We really needed a miracle!

One day, I received a phone call from the Appala-chian Conference office. Larry Meadors, the Mission Director, asked if we would be interested in a team from South Carolina coming to the Big 4 P.H. Church to do repairs. The team consisted of skilled men and women in the area of house repairs. They generally went overseas each spring or summer. However, due to the COVID-19 restrictions, they were not able to do a mission trip overseas that year.

Larry connected us with Dawn and Brad Morris of Hickory Grove International Pentecostal Holiness Church. They were the Missions Directors. After speaking with my husband about the repair needs, they committed to come.

I called Dawn, the Nehemiah from South Carolina. She was truly gifted at evaluating the damages of older buildings. And she was able to calculate the materials, manpower, and cost to turn an old building into a novel piece of real estate.

This team spent well over $10,000 to overhaul the Big 4 P.H. Church. I remember the summer day they came. The first time, they brought over 10 people to work on the church and had one week to tackle the task. The people were dedicated. Several of them took personal vacation days just to be at this West Virginia church. Some of the participants were in their 70s and 80s. But age did not slow them down. The church received new bathrooms, a new kitchen, a new stove, and a new sink. The outside of the building received fresh paint.

They were not able to complete the entire process, so Dawn scheduled the team to come again in the fall. On the second trip, everything was completed and money was provided to hire a roofer. The insurance company was amazed. The church received insurance coverage!

NAME OF THE BIG 4 P.H. CHURCH

The Big 4 P.H. Church was named after the four major coal mines that operated in the area during the 1960s and several years thereafter. This occurred during the Coal Boom in McDowell County, WV.

When the coal mines shut down, the entire county suffered. Many people moved out of the region to find jobs. The economy struggled. Rebuilding the economy would involve bringing more jobs to the area, and that would take time. It is still happening even as I write.

WISDOM BUILDS THE HOUSE

As I prayed for the church repair miracle, a certain scripture caught my attention.

"Through (skillful and godly) wisdom a house (a life, a home, a family) is built. And by understanding it is established (on a sound and good foundation), And by knowledge its rooms are filled With all precious and pleasant riches" (Proverbs 24:3-4 AMP).

WISDOM WINS WARS

Not only does wisdom play a role in building houses, but it also wins wars and that includes spiritual battles. Spiritual warfare is inevitable. The apostle Peter warns that the Devil prowls around looking for people to devour. He instructs us that we must be prepared to resist. Wisdom is a weapon of resistance that has defeated the Enemy many times.

> *Be sober (well balanced and self-disciplined), be alert and cautious at all times. That enemy of yours, the devil, prowls around like a roaring lion (fiercely hungry), seeking someone to*

devour. But resist him, be firm in your faith (against his attack– rooted, established, immovable), knowing that the same experiences of suffering are being experienced by your brothers and sisters throughout the world. (You do not suffer alone.) (1 Peter 5: 8-9 AMP)

WISE BUT HARMLESS

Jesus taught his disciples to be wise as a serpent but harmless as a dove. Jesus demonstrated this principle several times as people accuse him falsely.

"Behold, I send your forth as sheep in the midst of wolves: be you therefore wise as serpents, and harmless as doves" (Matthew 10:16 KJV).

WISDOM WINS A CITY

In the book of Ecclesiastes, there is a story of a man's wisdom that saved a city.

> *There was a little city, and few men within it; and there came a great king against it, and besieged it, and built great bulwarks against it. Now there was found in it a poor wise man, and he by his wisdom delivered the city; yet no man remembered that same poor man.* (Ecclesiastes 9:14-15 KJV)

WISDOM SOLVES DIFFICULT PROBLEMS

Daniel was a prophet known for his wisdom. He was introduced to King Belshazzar as a man of great understanding.

King Belshazzar urgently needed answers. He had just thrown a party for a thousand of his nobles and wanted to impress his army. He thought of taking the gold and silver vessels from Jerusalem—these were sacred and holy vessels. In an act of arrogance, he used these gold and silver vessels to serve wine.

This decision brought swift judgment from God. While the king was drinking wine, suddenly, the fingers of a man's hand appeared and began writing on the wall. There was no body—just a hand holding a pen and writing on the wall. Clearly, it was a heavenly intervention.

Quickly, the king instructed his servants to bring a man with the ability to interpret the writing.

> *There is a man in your kingdom in whom is a spirit of the holy gods, and in the days of your father, illumination, understanding and wisdom of the gods were found in him. And King Nebuchadnezzar, your father your father the king, appointed him chief of the magicians, enchanters, Chaldeans and diviners. It was because an extraordinary spirit, knowledge and insight, clarify riddles, and solve complex problems were found in this Daniel, whom the king named Belshazzar. Now let Daniel be called and he will give the interpretation.* (Daniel 5:11-12 AMP)

You may recall the words that were written: "Mene, mene, tekel, upsharsin." Daniel provided the meaning of this heavenly message: "numbered, weighed, and divided."

The king was found to be deficient on the heavenly scales.

His kingdom would be conquered and divided, and given to the Medes and Persians (Daniel 5:24-31).

That very night, King Belshazzar was killed and King Darius the Mede conquered the nation.

Wisdom is a weapon for spiritual warfare. Through wisdom, strategies for victory are disclosed!

A WEAPON OF CHOICE
AGAINST ACCUSATION

Accusation is a fiery dart that Satan delights to fire. Most every committed Christian will face accusations from the Evil One. Satan will find people willing to falsely accuse those of strong faith. Some examples include:

- Satan accused God of lying to Eve in the Garden of Eden (Genesis 3:1-6).
- Potiphar's wife falsely accused Joseph of sexual sin. This accusation landed him in prison for a period of time (Genesis 39:7-20).
- Satan falsely accused Job of serving God for profit (Job 1:9-10, Job 2:4-5).
- Daniel – cast in the lion's den because he prayed (Daniel Chapter 6).
- False witnesses spoke against Stephen and he was stoned as a punishment (Acts 6:7-15).

I remember a time when I faced the evil dart of accusation. Someone at work was truly jealous of me and did not like the Christian faith, although I treated the person with great respect. Tension existed.

One day when I came to work, I found a notice that I had been written up. It was a trivial situation and was presented falsely. I decided to respond wisely. A scripture arose in my spirit.

"The heart of the righteous studies to answer: but the mouth of the wicked pours out evil things" (Proverbs 15:28 KJV).

As time went on, it became evident that the false write-up was worthless. The human resources department did not believe the matter and neither did anyone else. It did not cause me any real harm. I am thankful that I remained composed.

JESUS WINS

The religious leaders were insanely jealous of Jesus. They devised a scheme to trap Him in His speech.

They came to Jesus and told Him that they knew He was one who taught the way of God. Then they asked Him a question to trap Him.

"Tell us, therefore, 'What do you think? Is it lawful to give tribute (taxes) unto Caesar, or not?'" (Matthew 22:17 KJV).

Is it lawful to pay taxes? If Jesus had said no, then He could have invoked the wrath of Caesar. If He had said yes, He could have been considered a traitor by the people.

Divine wisdom flowed from His mouth.

"They say unto him, Caesar's. Then saith he unto them, Render therefore unto Caesar the things which

are Caesar's; and unto God the things that are God's" (Matthew 22:21 KJV).

The accusers were stunned. Scripture says that they marveled at His wisdom (Matthew 22:22).

PRAY FOR WISDOM

Wisdom is available for the situations that you face. It is released to you when you ask for it. Pray this prayer from the book of Ephesians.

> *That the God of our Lord Jesus Christ, the Father of glory, may give unto you the spirit of wisdom and revelation in the knowledge of him. The eyes of your understanding being enlightened, that you may know what is the hope of his calling, and what the riches of the glory of his inheritance in the saints.* (Ephesians 1:17-18 KJV)

Did you pray? Did you ask for wisdom?

GAME CHANGER SPIRITUAL WEAPONS

PART 2

A sure way to reach the heart of the heavens is with prayers of remembrance. Repeating God's Word to Him from a heart filled with faith is a game changer.

The Scriptures are filled with episode after episode of famous intercessors praying in such a manner. Not only is God reminded of His past interventions, but Satan also listens to these prayers. These types of prayers call attention to the defeats of the Devil.

"Remind Me (of your merits with a thorough report), let us plead and argue our case together. State your position, that you may be proved right" (Isaiah 43:26 AMP).

Recall the time when a vast army surrounded King Jehoshaphat. He was determined to seek the Lord about the threat. Bravely, he stood before the assembly of Judah and Jerusalem. His prayer sent several reminders to God.

King Jehoshaphat's prayer is a great example for people who are facing threats to themselves or their families.

"And said, O Lord God of our fathers, art not thou God in heaven? and rulest not thou over all the kingdoms of the heathen? and in thine hand is there not power and might, so that none is able to withstand thee?" (2 Chronicles 20:6 KJV).

The King reminds God that He is omnipotent and he

continues with this manner of praying.

"Art not thou our God, who didst drive out the inhabitants of this land before thy people Israel, and gavest it to the seed of Abraham thy friend for ever?" (2 Chronicles 20:7 KJV).

The sound of these words brought an explosion of power from the heavenlies. A spirit of confusion struck the invading army, and they killed each other. They literally destroyed themselves (2 Chronicles 20:23-25 KJV).

KING HEZEKIAH

King Hezekiah faced a similar situation. The King of Assyria sent a threatening letter to Hezekiah. Basically, the letter stated that the king and the people should surrender or suffer great consequences.

King Hezekiah took this ugly letter to the temple of God. He spread out this letter of doom before the Lord. His prayer reminded God of His omnipotence.

Hezekiah prayed before the Lord and said, "O, Lord, the God of Israel, who is enthroned above the cherubim (of the ark in the temple), You are the God, You alone, of all the earth, You made the heaven of the earth. O Lord, bend down Your ear and hear; Lord,

open Your eyes, and see: hear the
(taunting) words of Sennacherib, which
he has sent to taunt and defy the living
God. (2 Kings 19:15-16 AMP)

The response from heaven was impressive. That very night, the angel of the Lord appeared and struck down 185, 000 men of the Assyrian nation.

The threat against King Hezekiah and the nation ended with supernatural assistance!

THE BREASTPLATE OF REMEMBRANCE

The Old Testament confirms the importance of re-minding God. When Aaron entered the Holies of Ho-lies to offer prayer and repentance for the nation, he wore on his chest a breastplate covered with precious stones to symbolize each tribe. The breastplate was made of elaborate material and held twelve precious stones attached to the ephod.

On each shoulder of this breastplate were two square stones made of black onyx. Each of the 12 sons of Israel were inscribed on the stones. The twelve stones were arranged in four rows of three stones. They were arranged from right to left.

"So Aaron shall carry the names of the sons of Israel
(Jacob) in the breast-piece of judgment over his
heart when he enters the Holy Place, to bring them

in continual remembrance before the Lord" (Exodus 28:29 AMP).

Our prayers should be prayed from the heart and be reminders to God. Remind God of His greatness. Remind Him of the victories He performed in the past. Remind Him of the people for whom you are praying. Remind Him of the situations you face!

Jesus is doing this. He stands before the throne of God and reminds Him. He is the One who intercedes for us. Remember that the next time you think nobody is praying for you.

"Therefore He is able also to save forever (completely, perfectly, for eternity) those who come to God through Him, since He always lives to intercede and intervene on their behalf (with God)" (Hebrews 7:25 AMP).

THE STONES IN THE BREASTPLATE

The twelve precious stones were arranged in four rows. Each row contained three stones. The high priest wore this breastplate as he stood before the Lord in the Holy of Holies.

The top row consisted of the tribes of Judah, Issachar, and Zebulun. The tribe of Judah began the row located in the top left.

The stone for Judah appears to be a bright red ruby.

107

The Christian beliefs connect the red ruby stone with the sacrifice of the blood of Jesus upon the cross. Other scriptures speak of the value of rubies.

"For wisdom's profit is better than the profit of silver, And her gain is better than fine gold. She is more precious than rubies; And nothing you can wish for compares with her [in value]" (Proverbs 3:14-15 AMP).

The stone for the tribe of Issachar was a golden, yellow topaz stone. From age to age of time, topaz has been associated with wealth. The tribe of Issachar was known for their commitment to work.

Topaz is also mentioned in Ezekiel 28:13. The gemstone for Zebulun was a diamond. It reflects the sparkling light of the water and the sky. Jacob's prophecy refers to the dwelling of this tribe.

"Zebulun shall dwell at the haven of the sea; and he shall be a haven for ships, and his border shall be unto Zidon" (Genesis 49:13 KJV).

The symbolism of the diamond suggests purity and light. As a reminder, these three tribes were camped on the east side of the temple.

East is known as the sacred direction where the temple faced and the direction from which Christ will return (Matthew 24:27).

The second row started with the tribe of Dan located to the left.

The gemstone for the tribe of Dan was a sapphire. It was a beautiful blue color. The deep blue color of the sapphire represents the heavens. It refers to the qualities of loyalty, truth, and divine correction.

Naphtali is the middle tribe in this row. The gemstone was a delightful purple amethyst.

The tribe of Gad completes this row. Gad (amethyst) stone was colored orange jasper. Other scriptures suggest the obsidian stone.

These three tribes were located to the north of the temple. The third row consisted of the tribes of Reuben, Simeon, and Levi.

Reuben lies to the left of the breastplate. Its stone was an odem, red-ruby color. Ruby was the stone associated with this tribe.

In the middle of the row was the tribe of Simeon. A green topaz was the stone representing this tribe.

The last row included the tribes of Asher, Joseph, and Benjamin.

At the end of the row was the tribe of Levi. Levi's stone was an emerald with veins of white, black, and red. This priestly tribe had two additional stones known as Urim and Thummim. The stones were kept in a pocket behind the breastplate. They were used for those who sought guidance from the Lord (Exodus 28:30; 1 Samuel 22:18).

The stone of Urim represents the concept of guilt. The Urim stone was white. Whereas the stone of Thummim represented the concept of innocence. The Thummim stone was black. They were used by the Hebrew priests in the act of seeking knowledge from God.

On the fourth row were the tribes of Asher, Joseph, and Benjamin. Asher was located to the left of the breastplate. Asher's stone was beryl. In the Bible, the color was considered to be sea green (Exodus 28:20, 18:13 KJV).

The tribe of Joseph was in the center of the row. Malachite was the stone. The color was black. Finally, the tribe of Benjamin was at the far end of the breastplate. Opal was the stone for this tribe. It represented the ability to bring unity and peace.

SYMBOLISM OF THE STONES

Jacob prophesied over each tribe shortly before his death.

"And Jacob called unto his sons, and said, Gather yourselves together, that I may tell you that which shall befall you in the last days" (Genesis 49:1 KJV).

JUDAH

Ruby is the color of stone associated with the tribe of Judah. Praise and thanksgiving reflect the meaning of this stone. Consider the power of praise. A powerful weapon of spiritual warfare is seen with this stone.

"Judah, thou art he whom thy brethren shall praise: thy hand shall be in the neck of thine enemies; thy father's children shall bow down before thee" (Genesis 49:8 KJV).

This was a tribe noted for offering praise and thanksgiving to the Lord. Praise is a weapon of spiritual warfare.

Recall the story of King Jehoshaphat during the battle with Moab. The instructions from the Lord were to send singers before the army (2 Chronicles 20:18 -22).

In addition, the ruby stone was known as the leader of precious stones. Judah was the leader during military battles!

ISSACHAR

Topaz was associated with this tribe. The prophecy of Jacob states that Issachar is a strong donkey couching between two burdens (Genesis 49:14).

Issachar was the fifth son of Leah. His name means work, hire, or reward. It refers to Leah paying a wage of mandrakes to her sister Rachel whose job was to have a night with Jacob. Thus, Issachar was born.

Notice the mention of two burdens. A spiritual meaning to be conferred relates to Jesus. One side of the burden was that Christ paid the price for the wages of death. On the other side, He was rewarded to His believers.

"He shall see of the travail of his soul, and shall be satisfied: by His knowledge shall my righteous servant justify many, for he shall bear their iniquities" (Isaiah 53:11 KJV).

Topaz is a soft type of stone. It must stay polished to protect its luster. Likewise, we must spend precious time in God's presence, lest we lose our zeal. We must make the time for prayer.

ZEBULUN

From Jacob's prophecy, we are told that this tribe lived by the sea (Genesis 49:13). The diamond was the gemstone of Zebulun. When the light of the sun

113

shines over the sea, it reflects the beauty of this stone. When God's light shines upon us, we also reflect His glory. Abiding with God causes us to shine. Moses illustrated this fact when he came down from Mount Sinai, and his face shined (Exodus 34:29 KJV).

Jesus told His disciples that they were to let their light shine:

"Let your light so shine before men, that they may see your good works, and glorify your Father which is in heaven" (Matthew 5:26 KJV).

DAN

Sapphire is the gemstone of the tribe of Dan. Jacob's prophecy provides great insight into this tribe.

"Dan shall judge his people, as one of the tribes of Israel. Dan shall be a serpent, by the way, an adder in the path, that bites the horse heels, so that his rider shall fall backward" (Genesis 49:16-17 KJV).

The Bible connects the meaning of the sapphire stone with truth, honesty, and bringing correctness. Christian religion associates sapphires with repentance.

NAPHTALI

This tribe was noted for the help that they provided to the nation of Israel to conquer the land of Canaan (Judges 4:4-10). Naphtali was the eighth son of the family.

Amethyst was the gemstone for this tribe. This beautiful, purple crystal has spiritual meaning. It is known as a spiritual protector. It provides spiritual and emotional protection. Inner peace is associated with the stone.

GAD

Certain scriptures indicate that the obsidian was the stone for this tribe. It was suggested that this stone provided protection from negativity. Certainly, this definition fits the tribe of Gad. These warriors protected the borders of Israel.

"And of Gad he said, Blessed be he that enlarges GAD: he dwells as a lion, and tears the arm with the crown of the head" (Deuteronomy 33:20 KJV).

REUBEN

Ruby represented the tribe of Reuben. It represented romantic love. It spoke of being faithful in a relationship. Reuben was the firstborn son of Jacob. This tribe dwelt on the eastern side of the Jordan and shared a border with Moab.

SIMEON

The green topaz shone on the breastplate of this tribe. Friendship and happiness are associated with this stone. The tribe of Simeon is mentioned with the tribe of Levi as those who hurt others with their

115

swords. Simeon was noted to be very fearless yet envious. He was antagonistic toward Joseph.

LEVI

This gemstone was an emerald with veins of white, black, and red.

Levi was the third son of Jacob. Some of the famous people from this tribe include Moses and Aaron. The tribe of Levi were mostly members of the priesthood. They cared for the Jewish temple. They also served in temple duties that included musicians, gatekeepers, judges, and craftsmen (Numbers 1:48-53).

ASHER

Chrysolite, of a gold color, is thought to be a gemstone. The symbol of this tribe was an olive tree, which brought wealth. Leah named Zilpah's second son, Asher. The abundance of fortune and joy was indicated by this name. This tribe provided an abundance of wheat, barley, grapes, figs, pomegranates, olives, and dates.

"Out of Asher his bread shall be fat, and he shall yield royal dainties" (Genesis 49:20 KJV).

JOSEPH

Black onyx was known as the gemstone for this tribe. Other scriptures suggest that it was black and white and sometimes brown. It gave reference to marital happiness.

This tribe was known for Joseph's dream of ears of corn. Joseph was known for his gift of interpreting the dreams of Pharoah. A future famine was the topic of the dream (Genesis 40:1-13).

BENJAMIN

The jasper stone was thought to be the gemstone for this tribe. This was the 12th stone of the breastplate. It is noted for its clear luster. It is considered to be a powerful healing stone.

Even though Benjamin was the youngest of the tribes, it was noted for providing spiritual, and political leadership. Strength was a characteristic of this tribe.

"Benjamin shall raven as a wolf: in the morning he shall devour the prey, and at night he shall divide the spoil" (Genesis 49:27 KJV).

GEMSTONES OF THE
BREASTPLATE DIFFERENCES

Scriptures speak of these stones; however, interpretations of the stones appear to vary. Some key reference scriptures for the breastplate gemstones include:

- Exodus 28:15-27

- Exodus Chapter 39
- Ezekiel 28:17-20
- Leviticus 8:6-10

CONNECTING THE GEMSTONES
PAST—PRESENT—FUTURE

As the high priest prayed in the Holy of Holies, the breastplate of gems gleamed in the light of the candles. Heaven looked down upon his prayers and offerings. The tribes were brought before God and reminded Him of His people and His covenant with them.

Prayers of remembrance touched the heart of God and brought forth the hand of heaven to aid the nation of Israel!

As He suffered on the cross, Jesus cried out, "It is finished." Then He bowed His head and gave up the ghost (John 19:30 KJV).

Unusual events occurred after these words and His death. The heavy veil of the temple was torn from top to bottom. That veil was four inches thick. It was said to be as thick as a man's hand (Exodus 26:31-37).

Descriptions from Scripture suggest that the veil was 30 feet in width and 60 feet in length.

The sheer size of the veil required about 300 priests

to maneuver it. Now this veil standing between death and life was torn by a supernatural force! (Luke 23:44-47).

The ark of intercession has changed. Jesus stands before the Father in heaven and intercedes for us. We are considered temples of the Holy Spirit and living stones. We are to stand before the Father in heaven and present the struggles of others before the throne of God.

"Do you not know and understand that you (the church) are the temple of God and that the Spirit of God dwells (permanently) in you (collectively and individually)? (1 Corinthians 3:16 AMP).

Jesus is praying for us. He reminds the Father in heaven that we have been redeemed by His blood.

"Therefore He is able also to save forever (completely. Perfectly, for eternity) those who come to God through Him, since He always lives to intercede and intervene on their behalf (with God)" (Hebrews 7:25 AMP).

Not only are we considered temples that God's Spirit dwells in, but we are also called living stones. We are stones that stand before God. We shine in His presence. Prayers of intercession flow from these living stones. We cry out to God for the souls of mankind!

"You (believers), like living stones, are being built up into a spiritual house for a holy and dedicated priesthood, to offer spiritual sacrifices (that are) acceptable and pleasing to God through Jesus Christ" (1 Peter 2:5 AMP).

We are precious in His sight. Our prayers are of great value in the ears of heaven. Many things would never happen if we fail to pray.

Look forward to the future from the book of Revelation. When the end-time events are nearly completed, a new Jerusalem descends from heaven. This heavenly city has twelve gates that give reference to the twelve tribes (Ezekiel 48:30-35; Revelation 21:12).

The heavenly city also has twelve foundation stones that may refer to the twelve apostles (Ephesians 2:20). There they are—the precious gemstones.

The foundation stones of the wall of the city were adorned with every kind of precious stone. The first foundation stone was jasper, the second sapphire: the third, chalcedony: the fourth, emerald. The fifth, sardonyx: the sixth, sardius: the seventh, chrysolite (yellow topaz): the eighth, beryl: the ninth, topaz: the tenth, chrysoprase: the eleventh, jacinth: the twelfth, amethyst. (Revelation 21:19-20 AMP)

120

HEART GEMS

The high priest wore the breastplate of gems as He entered the Holy of Holies to stand before the Lord. These gems were close to his heart. This heart location symbolized that each tribe was loved in the presence of the Lord.

"And, thou shalt put in the breastplate of judgment the Urim and the Thummim; and they shall be upon Aaron's heart, when he goes in before the Lord: and Aaron shall bear the judgment of the children of Israel upon his heart continually" (Exodus 28:30 KJV).

THE HEART OF JESUS

Jesus is now the High Priest and sits at the right hand of the throne of God. He makes intercession (prays) for the people. His blood was carried to the mercy seat in heaven and provides forgiveness for all that receive Him. On the other hand, Jesus holds His priesthood permanently and without change because He lives forever.

"Therefore He is able to save forever (completely, perfectly for eternity) those who come to God through Him, since He always lives to intercede and intervene on their behalf (with God)" (Hebrews 7:24-25 AMP).

SPIRITUAL WARFARE FROM THE HEART

Prayers released from the heart with confidence and faith are proven weapons of warfare. Elijah is one example. His prayers called down fire from heaven. They included praying God's Word and promises, as well as reminding God of His omnipotence!

If you want to see answers to prayer then model your prayers according to the following scripture:

> *Therefore, confess your sins to one another (your false steps, your offenses), and pray for one another, that you may be healed and restored. The heartfelt and persistent prayer of a righteous man (believer), can accomplish much (when put into action and made effective by God---it is dynamic and can have tremendous success.* (James 5:16 AMP)

6

PROPHESY TO THE WIND

"Then said he unto me, Prophesy unto the wind. Thus saith the Lord God. Come from the four winds. O breath, and breathe upon these slain, that they may live" (Ezekiel 37:8 KJV).

Prophecy is an effective weapon for spiritual warfare. You may question the connection of prophecy to the pillar of fire by night and the pillar of cloud by day.

The answer is simple. Moses was one of the greatest prophets mentioned in the Bible. Both the fire and cloud were prophetic signs that gave guidance to the nation of Israel. Likewise, prophecy gives direction to our lives. The fire and cloud were deterrents to the enemies of the nation of Israel. And for us, prophecy strikes fear in the hearts of our enemies.

I recall the first time I met a prophet. Although I believed in the gifts of the Spirit, I had never had an encounter with a prophet. Yes, God gives us gifts, and prophecy is one of those gifts.

Having then gifts differing according to the grace that is given to us, whether prophecy, let us prophesy according to the proportion of faith. Or ministry, let us wait on our ministering: or he that teaches, on teaching.

*Or he that exhorts, on exhortation: he
that gives, let him do it with simplicity.
He that rules, with diligence, he that
shows mercy, with cheerfulness. Let
love be without dissimulation, Abhor
that which is evil; cleave to that which
is good.* (Romans 12:6-9 KJV)

My knowledge of prophecy was based on God's
Word. Clearly, prophecy is a gift that operates with
faith. Also, prophecy should be used to assist the
body of Christ. Finally, God's love must dwell in the
person who prophesies.

WOMEN'S AGLOW

An invitation was sent to me to attend a Women's
Aglow meeting. At that time, my husband and I were
attending a Pentecostal Church and we really enjoyed the services. We could feel God's presence during the music services and when the preacher delivered the message, the Word of God seemed to come
alive to me. Finally, the altar services were so helpful
to me. During these altar times, people prayed for me
and whatever need I experienced, prayer was made.
However, I had never seen a prophet before. The
friend who invited me to the Women's Aglow meeting told me that a powerful prophetess would be
speaking. When I arrived at the meeting, I found a
seat close to the front because I did not want to miss

anything.

The service began with several songs being sung, and then the prophetess stood up and took the microphone. She was filled with boldness, and her eyes darted about the room. Then she preached a powerful message. Suddenly, she shifted from preaching to prophesying! She began to speak words of life over people, and everything she spoke came straight from the Scriptures. I looked up and she was standing right in front of me. Her fiery eyes were looking right through my soul. I nodded my head to confirm that I wanted her to pray for me.

As I recall, the encounter went like this: she laid her hands on my head and told me to look up. She instructed me to keep my eyes open, and then she began to pray over me. The power of God's presence was so strong that I struggled to stay on my feet. Then it seemed as if she had read my very soul. "You have been seeking an experience with God. You want to be filled with His peace and His power," she said. Then she spoke scriptures to confirm her message.

I liked that. I strongly believe that everything we say in the ministry should be guided by God's scriptures. "Seek ye the Lord while he may be found, call ye upon Him while he is near" (Isaiah 55:6 KJV).

I became a different person after that encounter. My

commitment to follow God's purposes was strengthened!

THE GIFT IMPARTED

Could prophecy be for me?

At seventeen, great challenges confronted me. Some things grieved me and caused me stress. These challenges led me to seek God and not run from Him. I attended a Bible study group that met each morning before school started. I asked a few of the students to pray for me. They laid hands upon me and prayed.

The light of prophecy would find me. It shined for me during a dark time of my life. As the students prayed, darkness lifted off me. A peace that I had never known until this moment settled upon my heart and mind!

Experiencing the presence of God at this young age brought me great comfort and assurance. When I prayed, I felt His presence and often saw answers for what I was praying.

One particular scripture described the significance of the experiences of God's presence after the students prayed.

"So we have the prophetic word made more certain. You do well to pay (close) attention to it as to a lamp shining in a dark place, until the day dawns and light breaks through the gloom and the morning star

arises in your hearts" (2 Peter 1:19 AMP).

LAYING ON OF HANDS

Scriptures tell of the impartation of spiritual gifts through the laying on of hands. However, this process works both ways. Those who lay their hands in prayer must be filled with faith and God's love. Similarly, the seeker must also have faith and pure motives.

Several times, hands were laid upon me for the impartation of ministry gifts. Some of these times included:

- Laying on hands at a Women's Aglow meeting
- Imparting blessings through the laying on of hands during the Night Watch prayer meeting
- Laying on hands at my ministry ordination service

This service was described in detail in my first book, *In Your Light We See Light.*

Apostle Paul addresses this practice of laying on of hands.

"Neglect not the gift that is in thee, which was given thee by prophecy, with the laying on of hands of the presbytery" (1 Timothy 4:14 KJV).

PROPHESY TO THE DRY BONES

How did Ezekiel react when the hand of God carried him to a Valley of Dry Bones? He reported that there were very many bones lying in the open valley. And he emphasized that these bones were very dry (Ezekiel 37:1-2).

"Can these bones live?" This was the question that the Lord asked Ezekiel (Ezekiel 37:3).

Despite what he saw, the prophet answered wisely:

"And He said to me, 'Son of man, can these bones live?' And I answered, 'O Lord God, You know'" (Ezekiel 37:3 AMP).

This answer from the prophet has taught me much about prayer. I have learned that no matter how impossible the situation appears, I must pray. I must acknowledge that God knows. He knows. Yet, He requires prayer over impossible situations!

It was time for Ezekiel to act. He was instructed to prophesy to the bones.

"Again He said to me, "Prophesy to these bones and say to them, 'O dry bones, hear the word of the Lord" (Ezekiel 37:4 AMP).

Another lesson for spiritual warfare! Speak God's Word to the impossible situation.

This was a two-way street. Ezekiel prophesied as he was commanded and God responded:

"Thus says the Lord God to these bones, "Behold, I will make breathe enter you so that you may come to life" (Ezekiel 37:5 AMP).

Do not underestimate the value of praying God's Word over situations, people, and circumstances!

The power of God's Word is confirmed by Scripture.

> *For the word of God is living and active and full of power (making it operative, energizing, and effective). It is sharper than any two-edged sword, penetrating as far as the division of the soul and spirit (the completeness of a person), and of both joints and marrow (the deepest parts of our nature), exposing and judging the very thoughts and intentions of the heart.*
> (Hebrews 4:12 AMP)

The Lord caused those bones to live after His prophet prophesied as commanded.

The Lord continued to work with those bones. He put sinews on them and covered them with skin. Suddenly, there was a thundering noise as those bones came together.

Ezekiel looked upon these bones. They had sinews on them. Flesh and skin covered them. Truly, this was amazing. But God was not through. There was no breath in these bones.

Another valuable lesson is taught. As intercessors, we must not stop praying until the work is complete. God wanted to complete the work. Yet, a prophecy was required from the prophet.

Think about it: those bones would have stayed in that state unless a prophet did his job.

A new command is now seen! No longer does the prophet speak to the bones. He must prophesy to the wind.

"Then said he unto me, Prophesy unto the wind, prophesy, son of man, and say to the wind, Thus saith the Lord God; Come from the four winds, O breath, and breathe upon these slain, that they may live" (Ezekiel 37:9 KJV).

QUESTION

Why would God command Ezekiel to prophesy to the Spirit of God?

The Spirit of God works through the Word of God to reveal Christ. Therefore, we must pray and ask God to do His work through His Word! Ezekiel reminded God of His Word with prayer. This type of prayer is so powerful, and the results are clearly seen!

"Put me in remembrance: let us plead together; declare thou, that thou mayest be justified" (Isaiah 43:26 KJV).

"So, I prophesied as He commended me, and the breath came into them, and they came to life and stood up on their feet, an exceedingly great army" (Ezekiel 37:10 AMP).

Persevere in prayer until the job is complete!

MORE FACTS ABOUT PROPHECY

To prophesy means to speak as if divinely inspired. Prophecy is intended to build up the body of believers. It should be inspired by the Holy Spirit and generally communicates an encouraging message. Prophecy is greatly needed today. On one hand, words of prophecy activate the Holy Spirit, and on the other hand, words of prophecy intimidate the Evil One. Consider the time when Moses found himself overwhelmed.

"I am not able to bear all this people alone, because it is too heavy for me" (Numbers 11:14 KJV).

"And the Lord came down in a cloud, and spake unto

him, and took of the spirit that was upon him, and gave it unto the seventy elders: and it came to pass, that, when the spirit rested upon them, they prophesied, and did not cease" (Numbers 11:25 KJV).

The Spirit of prophecy was poured upon the elders!

WHEN THERE ARE NO PROPHETS

The hand of the Lord carried Ezekiel to a place where there were no prophets, thus, there was dryness and death! God's Presence departed from the nation of Israel prior to the arrival of Samuel. The effectiveness of Eli the priest had grown dim. The spiritual condition of the nation was so depressed that there was no open vision. And the Word of the Lord was rare (1 Samuel 3:1-3).

Conditions deteriorate when there is no longer a true prophet (Psalm 74:9). This chapter tells of devastation and attacks by enemies because there is no prophet. The people do not see the signs of God, so they cannot respond because there is no prophet!

"We see not our signs: there is no more any prophet: neither is there among us any that knows how long" (Psalm 74:9 KJV).

Moses was a prophet chosen by God to lead the children of Israel out of Egypt. His leadership was characterized by prophetic acts, prayers, and even words.

"And by a prophet the Lord brought Israel up from Egypt, and by a prophet he was preserved" (Hosea 12:13 KJV).

Not only did Moses lead as a prophet, but his brother Aaron was also known as a prophet.

> *Then the Lord said to Moses, "Now hear this: I make you as God to Pharaoh (to declare My will and purpose to him): and your brother Aaron shall be your prophet." "You shall Speak all that I command you, and your brother Aaron shall tell Pharoah to let the children of Israel go out of his land.* (Exodus 7:1-2 AMP)

NO PROPHET AND NO DELIVERANCE

For four hundred and thirty years, the children of Israel lived in the land of Egypt (Exodus 12:40). And if God had not sent a prophet to the Pharoah of Egypt, the children of Israel would have continued to live in bondage!

BONDAGE

Bondage is a ploy of the Devil. He will not let people out of his grip once they become entrapped. But deliverance can come by means of the prophetic anointing and words.

I have experienced it. I have seen loved ones and friends trapped in the following bondages:

- Peer pressure
- Discouragement
- Debt
- Drugs
- Despair
- Divorce

Our prayer group was called to pray for several friends. We had to pray God's Word and purposes into their lives. They were following the Devil's purposes.

"Turn around and get out of bondage." Those words are easy to say to a captive of Satan. But the power to break away from bondage is often lacking. However, the course of their lives can be turned as intercessors pray God's Word into their situation.

Such prayers may be prophetic as they are called out of darkness into the light of God. People must pray for God's light to shine into their lives. Otherwise, they will continue to live in darkness.

"For God who said, 'Let light shine out of darkness,' is the One who has shone in our hearts to give us the Light of the knowledge of the glory and majesty of God (clearly revealed) in the face of Christ" (2 Corinthians 4:6 AMP).

I have seen people delivered from drugs, debt, and troubled marriages by prayers of this nature.

The light of God is very powerful when it is released by prayer. Consider the apostle Paul. Before his conversion, he was known as Saul. He was traveling on the road to Damascus, carrying letters from authorities to capture Christians and bring them to Jerusalem. There, they would be punished for their beliefs.

His travel plans were interrupted by a great light. From heaven, great beams of light flashed around him. The glory of God was displayed by this great light.

Off his horse, he fell to the ground. And the voice of the Lord spoke to him: "Saul, Saul, why are you persecuting and oppressing Me?" (Acts 9:4).

The Lord sent a disciple named Ananias to assist Saul. He had been blinded by the light and remained blind for three days. Someone had been praying for him. One of these intercessors could have been Stephen.

A group of men were displeased with the preaching of Stephen. With great rage, they drove him out of the city to be killed by stoning. Saul was present at this horrific event. The witnesses against Stephen placed their outer robes at the feet of Saul (Acts 7:58).

Stephen's last visions and words prior to his death were remarkable.

"And he said, 'Look! I see the heavens opened up (in welcome) and the Son of Man standing at the right hand of God!'" (Acts 7:56 AMP).

More than likely, Saul heard his last words.

"Then falling on his knees, (in worship), he cried out loudly 'Lord, do not hold this sin against them (do not charge them)!' When he said this, he fell asleep, in death" (Acts 7:60 AMP).

THE PLAGUES OF EGYPT

Going back to the example of Moses operating in the prophetic anointing, his words and actions allowed the release of the various plagues.

A review of the first plaque confirms the power of deliverance from his prophetic acts and words.

WATER TURNED TO BLOOD

The Lord told Moses to go to Pharaoh in the morning. Moses was to wait for him at the bank of the Nile River. As Pharaoh approached the river, he intended to acknowledge the god of the Nile. The Egyptians worshipped the god of the Nile, Hapi. Unexpectedly, he encountered a prophet who served the God of Moses, known as Yahweh.

With prophetic words from God, Moses greeted the Pharaoh.

"You shall say to him, "The Lord, the God of the Hebrews, has sent me to you, saying, "Let My people go, so that they may serve Me in the wilderness. But behold, you have not listened until now" (Exodus 7:16 AMP).

Those words from God were released from the mouth of Moses to bring forth actions from the heavenly realm. Next, actions for Moses added to the demonstration of God's power.

> *Then the Lord said to Moses, "Take your staff and stretch out your hand over the waters of Egypt, over their rivers, over their streams, over their pools, and over all their reservoirs of water, so that they may become blood: and there shall be blood throughout all the land of Egypt, in containers both of wood and stone."*
> (Exodus 7:19 AMP)

Moses and Aaron did as the Lord commanded. They not only spoke God's words, but they also acted as God instructed.

"So Moses and Aaron did as the Lord commanded; Aaron lifted up the staff and struck the waters in the

Nile, in the sight of Pharoah and in the sight of his servants, and all the water that was in the Nile was turned to blood" (Exodus 7:20 KJV).

For seven days, this plague of blood upon the Nile lasted.

The pattern of prophetic acts and words was performed until deliverance finally came!

PROPHETIC PRAYERS OF MOSES

The value of prophetic prayers is priceless in the eyes of heaven. Such prayers can bring deliverance when nothing else works!

At one point, the children of Israel grieved the Lord with their sins and idolatry so much that He was ready to take action.

> *The Lord said to Moses, "How long will these people treat me disrespectfully and reject Me? And how long will they not believe in Me, despite all the (miraculous) signs which I have performed among them." I will strike them with the pestilence (plague) and dispossess them, and will make you into a nation greater and mightier than they.* (Numbers 14:11-12 AMP)

Moses pleaded with prophetic prayers for the

children of Israel. He reminded God of how He protected the nation with the pillar of cloud by day and the pillar of fire by night (Numbers 14:14). Moses pleaded on behalf of the children of Israel.

"Please pardon the wickedness and guilt of these people according to the greatness of Your loving-kindness, just as You have forgiven these people, from Egypt even until now" (Numbers 14:19 AMP).

Powerful was the prayer of Moses for these people.

"So the Lord said, 'I have pardoned them according to your word'" (Numbers 14:20 AMP).

Unless we pray, people will not be delivered or drawn to God!

PRAYER WALKING
FOR THE CHURCH IN TAZEWELL

As I stated in my first book, I participated in all-night prayer meetings at the Voice of Praise Worship Center in Bluewell, WV.

I was drawn by God's Spirit to these meetings. They were held on Friday nights, a couple of times a month (sometimes more often).

The prayer nights went by quickly. Before we knew it, dawn would approach. The presence of God was very strong in these prayer meetings. I noticed great victories in my life and my family after each prayer meeting.

Dreams that I had pursued for several years became reality after each prayer night. God's Spirit was truly working in my life and my family.

Often, we went on prayer missions. One of our missions was to pray all night for a church to be planted in Tazewell, Virginia.

One night, our prayer group arrived at the site. Here we were, ready to pray all night in a field for this church. There were some facilities for us to utilize if needed. The prayer leader was a godly man. He loved God and was a gifted intercessor. In addition, he had an excellent character.

He instructed us to put anointing oil on the bottom of our shoes. Then he led us around the land. We circled the plot several times and prayed for a church to be established. We prayed using the pattern of Moses. Prophetic words were spoken, and prophetic acts (prayer walking) were performed. We spoke life to that area. We prayed for a building to be erected. We prayed for a pastor and a congregation to come.

All night, we prayed for this church. We prayed for the finances to build the church, for future leaders of the church, and for the people of this region to be drawn to the church.

In a matter of two to three years of this all-night prayer event, a church named Destiny was built. Today, this church stands as a light to the community. It continues to flourish and thrive!

A PILLAR OF CLOUD BY DAY AND A PILLAR OF FIRE BY NIGHT

God's presence protected the children of Israel both day and night. The light of the cloud led and directed them as they traveled.

The pillar of fire protected them and allowed them to travel at night. Additionally, it served as a sign to the enemies of Israel. God assured them of His presence.

"He did not withdraw the Pillar of Cloud by day, nor the Pillar of Fire by night, from going before the people" (Exodus 13:22 AMP).

7

SIGNS AND WONDERS

The primary ways that we should be guided are by God's Word and His Spirit. However, many examples of signs and wonders are recounted in the Scriptures.

Signs and wonders have a strong impact on those who do not believe that Jesus is Lord. The hearts of kings were turned from worshiping pagan gods to honoring the true God, Yahweh! Also, the faith of intercessors is strengthened by the occurrence of signs and wonders. I can speak from experience on this issue. Signs and wonders help the intercessor hold on to God's promises during times of waiting for answers to prayers.

Consider the prophet Daniel. He waited twenty-one days for his prayer to be answered. Yet, the angel told him that his prayer was heard in heaven the first day he prayed. The delay was caused by war in the heavens. During this period, Daniel received an angel to assure him that he would see answers. The angel told Daniel that his prayers were heard.

Have you ever wondered if your prayers were heard?

"Then he (angel) said unto me, "Fear not, Daniel: for from the first day that thou did set thine heart to understand, and to chasten thyself before God, thy words were heard, and I am come for thy words" (Daniel 10:12 KJV).

Next, the angel addressed the delay.

"But the prince of the kingdom of Persia withstood me, one and twenty days; but lo, Michael, one of the chief princes, came to help me; and I remained there with the kings of Persia" (Daniel 10:13 KJV).

The reference was made to angelic and demonic spirits waging war over certain territories.

I NEEDED A SIGN

As I mentioned in my first book, there was a period of time when I led a monthly prayer meeting consisting of several churches in the community. We came together in unity to pray for the community. The presence of God in those prayer meetings was so precious. The atmosphere was charged with faith and victory. We experienced many personal victories, even as we prayed for the region.

It was not uncommon for people to experience healing. Some received words of knowledge that spoke directly to their hearts. Still, others saw loved ones come to the saving knowledge of Jesus. I organized these meetings and set an agenda with the assistance of others. All pastors received prayer. All were encouraged to participate. However, there were intense periods of spiritual warfare.

At times, attempts were made to interrupt or stop the meetings. But they were held and not canceled. There were challenges; yet, the intercessors remained devoted.

One night, after returning from a prayer meeting, I was exhausted and had to lie down on the couch. I closed my eyes, but I was not asleep. I was hoping to muster up enough strength to fix supper. Suddenly, I sensed a presence near me. I felt no fear.

I opened my eyes and saw a very large angel whose presence I sensed. I could feel his being close to me, and for a brief moment, I saw him. He had a sword and was clothed in brass-type garments. He was a war angel; I just knew that in my spirit. He reached out his hand and touched me on my right shoulder. After this, he left quickly. Indeed, this was a sign to me that not only strengthened my faith but also my body. Scriptures tell us that angels are ministering spirits! (Psalm 103:20).

REASONS FOR SIGNS & WONDERS

Signs and wonders were given in the Bible for several reasons.

1. To Warn People

   Consider Noah building the ark. His labor was a sign and a warning.

   "By faith Noah, being warned of God of things not seen as yet, moved with fear, prepared an ark to the saving of his house; by the which he condemned the world, and

became heir of the righteousness which is by faith" (Hebrews 11:7 KJV).

2. Execute Divine Judgment

   When the children of Israel marched around the walls of Jericho, their acts of obedience sent a message to that nation.

   "By faith, the walls of Jericho fell down, after they were compassed about seven days" (Hebrews 11:30 KJV).

3. Deliver People from Oppression

   Gideon's army was reduced to 300 men. This reduction was so God would receive the glory for the victory. His army received weapons of trumpets, empty pitchers, and lamps within the pitchers.

   "And the three hundred blew the trumpets, and the Lord set every man's sword against his fellow; even throughout all the host: and the host fled to Bethshittah in Zerapath, and to the border of Abe-meholah, unto Tabbath" (Judges 7:22 KJV).

4. To Mark Sacred Time

   Recall the time that Joshua fought against the

five kings of the Amorites (Joshua 10:5). Joshua's army was prevailing, but they needed more time. Soon, the darkness of the night would hinder their efforts.

Joshua prayed:

Then Joshua spoke to the Lord on the day when the Lord handed over the Amorites to the sons of Israel, and Joshua said in the sight of Israel, "Sun, stand still at Gibeon, And moon, in the Valley of Aijalon." So the sun stood still, and the moon stopped, Until the nation [of Israel] took vengeance upon their enemies. Is it not written in the Book of Jashar? So the sun stood still in the middle of the sky and was in no hurry to go down for about a whole day. (Joshua 10:12-13 AMP)

THE SIGN OF JONAH

There was a certain group of people whom Jesus said would not receive a sign. This was a group of highly educated priests who rejected Jesus. They made every effort to accuse Him. They wanted to prove that He was wrong. They did not care for the sick and suffering. They did not care that many lives were restored by Jesus!

One day, this group of critical scribes and Pharisees approached Jesus. They asked Him to show them a sign. Their demand for a sign was requested with the wrong motives.

Jesus saw the evil in their hearts. He discerned their wrong motives. Quickly, He responded with a strong rebuke.

> *But he answered and said unto them, An evil and adulterous generation seeketh after a sign; and there shall no sign be given it, but the sign of the prophet Jonah. For as Jonah was three days and three nights in the whale's belly; so shall the Son of man be three days and three nights in the heart of the earth.* (Matthew 12:39-40 KJV)

Jesus also addressed their reluctance to repent.

When Jonah preached to the city of Nineveh, the entire city repented. The time will come when this generation will condemn these skeptical scribes and Pharisees!

It appears that this generation had a greater accountability to believe because Jesus was among them. Jesus was a greater teacher and prophet than Johnah. Even as Jonah was in the belly of the whale for three days and nights, Jesus would be in the heart of the earth.

Doubt, unbelief, and lack of repentance are doors that block the release of signs.

SEVEN SIGNS OF JESUS

Even though Jesus performed numerous miracles, seven signs stand out.

1. Changing the water into wine at the wedding in Cana was the first sign.

   "This beginning of miracles did Jesus in Cana of Galilee and manifested forth his glory, and his disciples believed in him" (John 2:11 KJV).

2. Jesus healed the nobleman's son. His son was sick in the region of Capernaum. The child was close to death. The power of the Word of Jesus was seen.

   "Jesus said unto him, Go your way; your son lives. And the man believed the Word that Jesus had spoken unto him and he went his way" (John 4:50 KJV).

   The man's servant met him as he traveled. He told him that his son was alive. He was healed at the same hour that Jesus spoke the Word (John 4:53).

3. Healing of the man at the Pool of Bethesda (John 5:1-9).

I must say, this is one of my favorites. The scene occurred at the Pool of Bethesda that had five porches. Many people with all kinds of illnesses and afflictions lay around the pool. They were waiting for an angel to touch the pool. At a certain season, an angel would come and trouble the pool, and the first person to enter would be healed (v. 4).

Jesus engaged in a conversation with a man who suffered an infirmity for 38 years! (v. 5) Jesus asked him if he wanted to be made whole (v. 6). The man explained that he did not have anyone to help him in the pool. Someone always got there before him! I think he expected Jesus to help him get in the pool. But Jesus had a better idea. The living water of the Holy Spirit would heal him. Jesus told him, "Rise, take up your bed, and walk" (John 5:8 KJV). Immediately, the man was healed!

4. Feeding the 5000 people was another sign. (John 6:1-14). A little boy gave Jesus his lunch. Jesus gave thanks over the food. He broke the five loaves of barley bread and the two fishes and filled basket after basket (v. 9-13).

5. Jesus walking on water was a sign (John 6:15-21).

6. Healing the blind man from birth was another sign and a miracle (John 9:1-13).

7. Raising Lazarus from the dead was a great sign and wonder. For four days, he had been dead in the grave. But Jesus prayed to His Father. In a loud voice, He cried out: "Lazarus, come forth" (John 11:43 KJV). This sign turned the hearts of many Jews. Many of them believed in Him (John 11:45).

EYES AGAINST EYES VISION

When we find ourselves as targets of spiritual warfare, signs and wonders will help us stand strong in the faith. For about six months, a certain person treated me with great disrespect. However, I chose to respond courteously and just brush off the ugly words and actions. I am so glad that I kept my composure and stayed in peace.

I remembered the scripture that says we do not fight against flesh and blood. Our fight is against principalities, powers, rulers of the darkness of this world, and against spiritual wickedness in high places. (Ephesians 6:12). We are instructed to put on the entire armor of God, to pray and watch (Ephesians 6:13-20).

As I prayed about the matter, it appeared that the spirits of jealousy and resentment were the root causes of the actions displayed toward me.

I have learned that when the Holy Spirit exposes a spirit, that victory is on the way. Once the light of the Spirit begins to reveal motives, the evil tide starts to turn. During prayer, I sensed a battle between two sets of eyes. Now, this was not seen just once, but several times during many months.

The eyes of the spirit of jealousy shot forth evil rays. When these rays struck something, damage was inflicted. I searched for scriptures to give insight and confirmation because Scripture has a lot to say about eyes. The prophet Ezekiel describes an encounter with the image of jealousy.

> *And he put forth the form of a hand, and took me by a lock of mine head; and the spirit lifted me up between the earth and the heaven, and brought me into the visions of God to Jerusalem, to the door of the inner gate, that looks towards the north; where was the seat of the image of jealousy, which provokes jealousy. And behold, the glory of the God of Israel was there, according to the vision that I saw in the plain. Then said he unto me, Son of man, lift up your eyes now the way toward the north. So, I lifted up my eyes the way toward the north, and behold northward at the gate of the altar this image of jealousy in the entry.* (Ezekiel 8:3-5 KJV)

Yes, those eyes of jealousy shot forth fiery, evil rays that could be felt. But there were other eyes. The eyes of Jesus shot back rays of fire that crumbled the rays of jealousy. John saw a vision of Jesus on the Island of Patmos during his time of exile. He describes the eyes of Jesus.

"His head and his hairs were white like wool, as white a snow, and his eyes were as a flame of fire" (Revelation 1:14 KJV).

What I saw during times of prayer were battles between two sets of eyes. But every battle was won by the eyes of Jesus! It was not long after this that the situation against me just disappeared. As suddenly as the evil came, it left!

EYES OF THE ENEMY

The Enemy is watching us. He tries to catch us at weak moments. He attempts to entrap us. We must be alert and cautious.

King Hezekiah was considered a righteous king of the nation of Israel. He enacted religious reforms such as restoring the Passover celebrations and requiring the worship of Yahweh. He removed idols and forbade the worship of them.

"He trusted in the Lord God of Israel; so that after him was none like him among all the kings of Judah, nor any that were before him" (2 Kings 18:5 KJV).

However, King Hezekiah made a mistake by letting the eyes of the enemy see the great treasures of his house.

Foreign dignitaries visited him. The purpose of the visit appeared to be an effort to show goodwill. They heard that the king had been sick. They sent letters and presents to him.

This visit was not as innocent as it seemed. For some reason, King Hezekiah showed them all the treasures of his house, including the gold and silver, and the precious anointment. There was nothing in his house that he did not show these foreign leaders (2 Kings 20:13).

The prophet Isaiah came and asked the king about this visit. King Hezekiah told the prophet that the dignitaries were from Babylon.

Isaiah asked the king what he showed them.

"All the things that are in my house have they seen: there is nothing among my treasures that I have not shown them" (2 Kings 20:15 KJV).

King Hezekiah's decision to reveal all his treasures to these foreigners proved to be a serious error. Instead of celebrating the king's good fortune, jealousy and envy immediately took hold in their hearts. Isaiah responded to this with a warning!

"Behold, the days come, that all that is in thine house, and that which thy fathers have laid up in store unto this day, shall be carried into Babylon, nothing shall be left, saith the Lord" (2 Kings 20:17 KJV).

SIGNS AND WONDERS FOR A PAGAN KING

The prophet Daniel became a ruler over the entire province of Babylon and the chief of the governors over all the wise men of Babylon during the reign of the pagan king named Nebuchadnezzar. He rose to power after giving an interpretation of one of the king's dreams (Daniel 2:40-49).

King Nebuchadnezzar became consumed with the task of building a huge golden image. His motive may have been to establish his authority. The image was 90 feet high and 9 feet wide.

The king commanded that all the people must bow and worship this image when they heard the sound of the music. Those who did not obey would be thrown into a fiery furnace (Daniel 3:9-12). However, three of Daniel's friends refused to worship the idol. The king became enraged at them and had soldiers take them to the burning fiery furnace. The fire was so hot that the soldiers who took them to the fire were killed.

The fire had no power over these men of faith. They walked in the fire and a fourth man joined them. This man was the Son of God (Daniel 3:25).

When the king saw this scene, he was amazed. He commanded that the men come out of the fire and that all of Israel worship the one true God.

Signs and wonders turned the heart of this pagan king.

> *Nebuchadnezzar the king, unto all people, nations, and languages that dwell in tall the earth; Peace be multiplied unto you. "I thought it good to show the signs and wonders that the high God had wrought toward me. How great are his signs! And how mighty are his wonders! His kingdom is an everlasting kingdom, and his dominion is from generation to generation.* (Daniel 3:1-3 KJV)

The message for us is that signs and wonders can turn the hearts of those in places of high authority!

GIDEON NEEDED A SIGN

Gideon lived during a time of great depression and oppression in the nation of Israel. Therefore, he needed confirmation to obey God.

Due to the sins of the nation of Israel, the Lord delivered them into the hand of Midian for seven years. The Midianites were cruel. They caused so much terror in the nation that the people hid in caves in the mountains. Whenever Israel planted their crops, this enemy destroyed the entire harvest.

"And Israel was greatly impoverished because of the Midianites: and the children of Israel cried unto the Lord" (Judges 6:6 KJV).

As a result of their prayers, the Lord sent a prophet to speak the miracle of deliverance to the nation. Then, an angel was sent to Gideon who was threshing wheat when the angel came.

"And the angel of the Lord appeared unto him, and said unto him, The Lord is with thee, thou mighty man of valor" (Judges 6:12 KJV).

Gideon informed the angel that his family was poor and he was the least in his father's house (Judges 6:15). Step by step, Gideon began to rise to the task of leading an army against the nation of Midian. But he needed confirmation. So, he asked God for a sign.

"Behold, I will put a fleece of wool in the floor; and if the dew be on the fleece only, and it be dry upon the earth beside, then shall I know that thou wilt save Israel by mine hand, as thou hast said" (Judges 6:37 KJV).

When Gideon woke up the next morning, it happened as he asked. He wrung the dew out of the fleece, but he needed more confirmation. This was no problem for God who appeared to be willing to show another sign.

"And Gideon said unto God, Let not thine anger be

hot against me, and I will speak but this once: let me prove, I pray you thee, but this once with the fleece; let it now be dry only upon the fleece, and upon all the ground let there be dew" (Judges 6:39 KJV).

God answered his request again. And this sign thrust him forward toward the purposes of God!

WHERE IS THE GOD OF ELIJAH?

Elisha had just watched his great mentor, Elijah, being caught up in a chariot of fire and horses of fire. A whirlwind carried him into heaven (2 Kings 2:11).

He picked up Elijah's mantle and stood by the river bank of the Jordan. Just a few moments earlier, Elijah had struck the river with his mantle and it divided, allowing them to walk on dry ground. Now, he was alone with the mantle. He followed the example of his mentor.

"And he took the mantle of Elijah that fell from him, and smote the waters, and said, Where is the Lord God of Elijah? And when he also had smitten the waters, they parted hither and thither: and Elisha went over" (2 Kings 2:14 KJV).

During this moment of solitude, he needed a sign. And God gave him one! All he had to do was ask!

167

WONDERS

God is a God of wonders. The book of Psalms speaks of many of them.

"We give thanks and praise to You, O God, we give thanks, for Your (wonderful works declare that Your) name is near; People declare Your wonders" (Psalm 75:1 AMP).

DELIVERANCE

God used wonders to deliver His people from the oppressive hand of the evil Pharoah!

"And the Lord brought us out of Egypt with a mighty hand and with an outstretched arm and with great terror (suffered by the Egyptians) and with signs and with wonders" (Deuteronomy 26:8 AMP).

TO BUILD THE CHURCH

The wonders of God helped the apostles build the early church. Wonders were answers to prayers.

"At the hands of the apostles many signs and wonders (attesting miracles) were continually taking place among the people. And by common consent they all met together (at the temple) in (the covered porch called) Solomon's portico" (Acts 5:12 AMP).

168

WHAT IS THE KEY?

Signs and wonders occurred as God's people prayed and asked for them. They asked in sincerity. They asked with the right motives. They asked with an attitude of faith!

Signs and wonders helped God's people fulfill His purposes! And they will do the same for you!

KEYS TO AN OPEN HEAVEN

8

The Scriptures refer to an open heaven as a portal from which episodes of revival, blessings, and outpourings of the Holy Spirit are released. Also, manifestations such as miracles and healings occur!

Under what is often called a portal of an open heaven, the Holy Spirit is released in great measure. People are filled with joy, peace, and the assurance of God's power.

A great example is when the Gentiles in Cornelius' household received an outpouring of God's Spirit.

"While Peter was still speaking these words, the Holy Spirit fell on all those who were listening to the message (confirming God's acceptance of Gentiles)" (Acts 10:44 AMP).

During such times, the presence of God is so powerful, and there is a great awareness that He is very near.

Breakthrough is another term associated with an open heaven. Answers to prayers seem to come quickly. People who are resistant to the gospel suddenly have a change of heart. Other people report seeing angels during these special times!

Now it shall be, if you diligently listen
to and obey the voice of the Lord your

God, being careful to do all of His commandments which I am commanding you today, the Lord your God will set you high above all nations of the earth. All these blessings will come upon you and overtake you if you pay attention to the voice of the Lord your God. (Deuteronomy 28:1-2 AMP)

The heavens opened at Jesus' baptism.

After Jesus was baptized, He came up immediately out of the water; and behold, the heavens were opened, and he (John) saw the Spirit of God descending as a dove and lightning on Him (Jesus) and behold, a voice from heaven said, "This is My beloved Son, in whom I am well-pleased and delighted!" (Matthew 3:16-17 AMP).

WHEN THE HEAVENS ARE BRASS

Likewise, the heavens can be closed over a person or a city, town, or region. This is clearly seen when Jesus visited the city of Nazareth. He taught in the synagogue, but his teaching was not accepted. The hearts of the people were closed to Him. Regardless of all the miracles and mighty acts Jesus did, these people did not believe in Him.

They suggested that He was just one of them, just like them. After all, he was a carpenter, the son of Mary. They even stated that his brothers and sisters were there among them. Scriptures state that they were offended by Him. Their disapproval blinded them to the reality that He was anointed by God as the Messiah (Mark 6:1-3).

The atmosphere over that region was hardened by unbelief. Jesus could not perform any mighty miracles because of the unbelief in that city.

"And He could not do a miracle there at all (because of their unbelief) except that He laid hands on a few sick people and healed them. He wondered at their unbelief" (Mark 6:5-6 AMP).

Sin and disobedience can cause closed heavens over a certain region. Several consequences of disobedience are mentioned in the book of Deuteronomy (Deuteronomy 28:15-68).

One of those consequences was a heaven-like brass.

"The heaven which is over your head shall be bronze (giving no rain and blocking all prayers): and the earth which is under you, iron (hard to plow and yielding no produce.)" (Deuteronomy 28:23 AMP).

Also, it will be helpful to review the King James Version.

"And thy heaven that is over thy head shall be brass, and the earth that is under thee shall be iron" (Deuteronomy 28:23 KJV).

A CHOIR OF ANGELS

For a period of about two years, I participated in all-night prayer meetings. These meetings were held about twice a month. Also, I helped lead a corporate prayer event that invited churches from the community to attend a prayer meeting once a month. During these meetings, all pastors were invited to pray, and prayers were offered for the community as well.

During these all-night prayer meetings and the corporate prayer meetings, I experienced open heavens. The Holy Spirit saturated the atmosphere, and people received healings. Many also experienced great peace and joy!

It was during this two-year period that I received several visions and heavenly experiences. One of these heavenly encounters included hearing a choir of angels.

One morning, I went to Voice of Praise Church at 9:00 a.m. It is interesting to note that this is the time of a New Testament Prayer Watch. I was supposed to meet with the pastor regarding a certain project.

I sat down in the lobby, alone in the church. The atmosphere was so peaceful. But suddenly, loud singing from the sanctuary broke the silence. How could that be?

There was nobody in the church, but the singing continued. It was so loud that I had to see for myself. I opened the sanctuary doors and looked inside.

No one was in the sanctuary, but at the ceiling, a choir was singing beautiful tunes. I couldn't see them, but I could tell that they covered about one-fourth of the sanctuary. They were not singing in English or any other language of other nations.

In a celestial chorus, an otherworldly language resounded. The angels, ablaze with joy, sang without pause, their eyes upon me. Amidst their harmonious song, a soft yellow radiance enveloped the entire area where the angelic choir stood.

This heavenly experience had a profound effect on me. It strengthened my faith and ignited my desire to become a more effective intercessor.

A scripture came to mind as I reflected upon the angel's choir.

"When the morning stars sang together and all the sons of God shouted for joy" (Job 38:7 AMP).

AN OPEN HEAVEN FOR CORNELIUS

Cornelius was truly a man who could effectively pray for open heavens. He has much to teach us about this topic. Cornelius was a Roman centurion in Caesarea. He was not a Jew, but he loved God. His great desire was for himself and his family to receive an outpouring of the Holy Spirit.

> *He possessed the qualities of an effective intercessor. Indeed, his prayers touched heaven! "Now at Caesarea there was a man named Cornelius, a centurion of what was known as the Italian Regiment." A devout man and one who, along with all his household, feared God. He made many charitable donations to the Jewish people, and prayed to God always.* (Acts 10:1-3 AMP)

178

From these Scriptures, it is clear that he was committed to prayer. He prayed on a consistent basis. Also, he was faithful in giving to the Jewish people. Most likely, these donations helped the poor and assisted with the needs of the synagogue. In addition to these qualities, he instructed his family in the worship of God (v. 2). Not only did the people take notice of his faithfulness; heaven also observed it.

"About the ninth hour (3:00 p.m.) of the day he clearly saw in a vision as angel of God who had come to him and said, "Cornelius!" (Acts 10:3 AMP).

The 3:00 p.m. hour was a well-known prayer watch of the New Testament. The heavens opened for Cornelius! What was he doing when the heavens opened? Praying during the designated prayer watch!

THE MESSAGE OF THE ANGEL

Cornelius was frightened and stared intently at him and said, "What is it, lord (sir)/" And the angel said to him, Your prayers and gifts of charity have ascended as a memorial offering before God (an offering made in remembrance of His past blessings) (Acts 10:4 AMP)

The angel plainly tells us that prayers and offerings were received as a memorial and came up before God.

HIS PRAYERS PAVED THE WAY

The prayers of Cornelius paved the way for the great outpouring of the Holy Spirit upon the Gentiles! Without his prayers and offerings, this great outpouring of the Holy Spirit may not have happened. But he did pray! And the Holy Spirit was poured out!

DIVINE CONNECTIONS

I have learned about the importance of praying for divine connections. When God brings the right people together, at the right place and the right time, great things happen!

In order for the Holy Spirit to be poured out upon these Gentiles, Peter was required to preach to them. He was the right person, and preaching about the purpose and plan of Jesus was necessary. God could bring both of these events together. All He needed was someone to pray and believe.

PETER'S VISION

Cornelius was instructed to send for Peter (Acts 10: 7). Peter agreed to come and traveled to the destination. He went to a house to rest and eat. While lunch was being prepared, he went to the top of the house to pray. There's that word again—"prayer." Notice that both parties prayed.

Peter prayed at noon. Suddenly, he fell into a trance

and the heavens opened.

"And he saw heaven opened, and a certain vessel descending unto him, as it had been a great sheet knit at the four corners, and let down to the earth" (Acts 10:11 KJV).

This heavenly sheet was filled with unclean animals as described by the Scriptures. The voice told him, "Kill the animals and eat" (Acts 10:13).

"This was done thrice: and the vessel was received up again into heaven" (Acts 10:16 KJV).

Peter responded that he had never eaten anything unclean in his entire life (Acts 10:14).

Heaven replied, "And the voice spoke unto him again the second time, What God has cleansed, that call not thou common" (Acts 10:15 KJV).

Peter recognized that God was willing to pour out the Holy Spirit upon the Gentiles also.

"And when Peter went, he preached to them, and the Holy Spirit fell upon the Gentiles in the household of Cornelius" (Acts 10:44-48 KJV).

KEYS TO THIS OPEN HEAVEN

Part of Peter's message is that God is not partial. What God does for one person, He will do for another!

"Then Peter opened his mouth, and said, of a truth I perceive God is no respecter of persons" (Acts 10:34 KJV).

KEYS TO UNLOCK BLESSINGS

- Devotion: Be fully devoted to God (Acts 10:2).
- Fear and Honor: Reverence God and honor Him.
- Persistent Prayer: Pray with unwavering commitment.
- Generosity: Give alms to the poor and support God's purposes (Acts 10:2).
- Divine Connections: Expect timely and purposeful connections.

Remember, there's an open heaven waiting for you!

ABOUT THE AUTHOR

Mary Donna Hankla is an intercessor who strongly believes that God is a waymaker. She believes in the power of effective prayers to release Heaven's power into present situations. "Thus says the LORD, which makes a way in the sea, and a path in the mighty waters" (Isaiah 43:16). Mary has faced challenging situations and difficult people, but she has also witnessed the victories that God has brought. She greatly appreciates her husband and son, Kenny and Chris Hankla, who provide vital support for her ministry.

For over 22 years, Donna has been an active minister with the International Pentecostal Holiness Church (IPHC) and is also an ordained minister. She serves in the Appalachian Conference as a pastor and director of the WIN prayer program (World-Wide Intercessory Network). She has led many prayer watches, including Night-Watch, 24-Hour Prayer Watch, and 21-Day Daniel Fast, for the church and conference. Donna has participated in the National Day of Prayer in Washington, D.C., for 15 years, as well as prayer events sponsored by the Capitol Hill Prayer Partners, led by Sara Ballenger, and Women's Aglow. She has also led prayer walks to key regions such as Mount Mitchell in North Carolina. Since 2007, Donna has been a pastor at the Big Four Church in Kimball, WV. Currently, she works with a community action group that assists pregnant mothers and children up to the age of three.

Mary Donna Hankla can be followed using the QR codes on the back of this book.

www.ingramcontent.com/pod-product-compliance
Lightning Source LLC
Chambersburg PA
CBHW060519130626
46553CB00002B/561